...DY MEMORIAL LIBRARY
SOUTHWESTERN UNIVERSITY
GEORGETOWN, TEXAS 78626

W9-ADR-348

DISTRIBUTED BY

NATIONAL WOMEN'S HISTORY PROJECT
Box 3716   Santa Rosa, CA 95402 (707) 526-5974

WITHDRAWN

Women Who Dared to Be Different

A TARGET BOOK

Women Who Dared to Be Different

Edited, with commentary by Bennett Wayne

GARRARD PUBLISHING COMPANY
CHAMPAIGN, ILLINOIS

Picture credits:

The All-Woman Transcontinental Air Race, Inc.: p. 165 (bottom)
The American Telephone and Telegraph Company: p. 6
The Bettmann Archive, Inc.: pp. 35, 164 (top)
Brown Brothers: pp. 9 (portrait), 41, 163 (top and bottom), 164 (bottom)
The Buffalo Bill Historical Center, Cody, Wyoming: p. 78
Cincinnati Public Library: p. 71
Culver Pictures, Inc.: p. 163 (middle)
Denver Public Library, Western History Department: p. 86
Erich Hartman of Magnum Photos, Inc.: p. 129
Nantucket Maria Mitchell Association: p. 95
National Aeronautics and Space Administration, Houston, Texas: p. 127
New-York Historical Society: pp. 20, 47
New York Public Library: p. 31 (both)
New York Public Library Picture Collection: p. 62
Old Print Shop, New York: p. 111
Radcliffe College: pp. 136, 141
Steve Schapiro from Black Star: p. 56 (right)
The Smithsonian Institution: p. 165 (top)
John Turner from Black Star: p. 90
United Press International: pp. 55 (left), 57 (both), 59, 83,
    91 (both), 93 (both), 126, 128, 131, 146 (bottom), 159 (both)
Vassar College Library: pp. 121, 104
WABC-TV: p. 55 (right)
Wide World Photos: pp. 92 (both), 146 (top), 153
Bill Winfrey from Black Star: p. 56 (left)

Copyright © 1973 by Garrard Publishing Company
All rights reserved. Manufactured in the U.S.A.
International Standard Book Number: 8116–4902–4
Library of Congress Catalog Card Number: 72–6802

C
920
W367w

Contents

198820

Sex: Female
Occupation: Unlimited

This girl is an installer for a telephone company. It was not always possible for a woman to be an installer. Once she might have worked in an office or at a switchboard—or stayed at home. But this young woman would not take no for an answer! Today she is one of the ever-growing group of women who are opening new doors. They are deep-sea divers, generals, and boxing reporters. They are members of the stock exchange, taxicab drivers, and judges. They are working in jobs that were once reserved "for men only."

Not all of these women attract as much attention as a lady installer or general. Many of them are quietly working in fields where once they could fill only less important jobs. Now training programs are opening up for them. And more people are beginning to agree that women should have a chance to compete for top-level jobs. Many women are doing just that —and succeeding.

This book is about some daring women who lived in an earlier day. Like the young woman in the picture, they refused to believe that they could not do a "man's job."

Here are the exciting life stories of Nellie Bly, a pioneer woman reporter; Annie Oakley, whose shooting ability became a legend; Maria Mitchell, one of the first woman astronomers; and Amelia Earhart, whose flying adventures earned her the respect of people all over the world. Here, too, are the brave-hearted women who followed in their footsteps.

This collection can be used as a springboard for the further study of women and their fight for equal rights in the United States. It can be read as history or as literature— but most especially, it should be read for pleasure.

NELLIE BLY
1867–1922

wrote to the editor of the *Pittsburgh Dispatch* when she was eighteen, declaring that women could do anything men could do—and do it better! Her letter resulted in Nellie's first job as a newspaper reporter! After a year or two as the *Dispatch*'s only girl reporter, Nellie headed for New York and the offices of *The World.* Here quick-thinking Nellie persuaded publisher Joseph Pulitzer to hire her. She was one of the newspaper world's first "sob sisters." Nellie interviewed factory workers, covered a hospital for the insane from inside its walls, and wrote about the life of a chorus girl. Her name became a household word in 1890 when she traveled around the world in less than eighty days—a record for that time—and sent home stories telling about her adventures. Nellie retired soon afterward, but not before she had blazed the way for the dozens of other women reporters who would follow in her footsteps.

Nellie Bly
Reporter for The World

by Charles P. Graves

Copyright © 1971 by Charles P. Graves

Elizabeth Cochrane

"Hey, Pinky!" Elizabeth Cochrane's brother shouted, slowing his horse. "I'll race you to the barn." Elizabeth, nicknamed Pinky for her favorite color, rode with her older brother almost every day.

"I'm ready!" Elizabeth yelled. "One, two, three, GO!" Elizabeth leaned low in her saddle and spurred her horse on. At first the two horses were neck and neck. Then slowly Elizabeth's horse pulled ahead.

"I won!" Elizabeth cried as she reined in her horse in front of the barn ahead of her brother.

"Aw, Pinky!" her brother complained. "Girls aren't supposed to beat boys at anything."

"There are lots of things that girls can do better than boys," Elizabeth said. "And I don't mean just cooking and sewing."

Elizabeth Cochrane, who would become famous as Nellie Bly, lived in Cochrane Mills, Pennsylvania. She had been born there in 1867. The little town, not far from Pittsburgh, was named after the mills owned by Elizabeth's father. He had been married twice, and there were six boys and four girls in his family.

Mr. Cochrane, who was a lawyer, had a large library, and he encouraged all his children to read. He taught Elizabeth to read and write when she was only a few years old.

Elizabeth enjoyed books. She had a strong imagination and, as she grew older, she often wrote stories to read to her friends. Elizabeth was popular, and the house was always full of children. "Tell us a story," they'd beg.

Elizabeth was proud of her stories. She would often lie awake in bed at night thinking up new plots.

"You're so much like your father," Mrs. Cochrane often said. "You're always thinking, thinking, thinking."

Elizabeth's father had died when she was nine. Since learning had been important to Mr. Cochrane, Elizabeth's mother wanted to see that his children got the best education available. She sent Elizabeth to a boarding school in the next county.

Elizabeth made good grades at the school, but she missed her family very much. Two years later she left the boarding school and continued her education at home.

One by one her older brothers moved to Pittsburgh and went to work there. When Elizabeth was eighteen, her brothers suggested that the entire family join them.

Elizabeth was delighted. Her father had not left much money, and Elizabeth wanted to earn some. She thought she would be able to find a better job in a big city like Pittsburgh than in a small town.

"What kind of job do you want?" Elizabeth's mother asked.

"Some people think I write well," Elizabeth said. "Maybe I can get a job on a newspaper."

Mrs. Cochrane laughed. "Few newspapers will hire women," she told her daughter. "Most editors believe that only men can write the news."

In those days many jobs were closed to women. Some girls worked in factories, but the pay was low and the work was hard. A few women were beginning to work in offices. Most men, however, believed that women could not understand business. In the 1800s women weren't even allowed to vote in elections.

No wonder Mrs. Cochrane didn't think much of Elizabeth's chances to get a job on a newspaper. However, Elizabeth was determined to try her luck in Pittsburgh.

Elizabeth Becomes Nellie Bly

Soon after Elizabeth arrived in Pittsburgh, she read an article in the *Pittsburgh Dispatch* called "What Girls Are Good For." The man who wrote it didn't think they were good for much. Girls should stay home and learn to keep house, he said.

As soon as Elizabeth read the article, she wrote a letter to the editor of the *Dispatch*. Her letter said that girls could do almost anything that boys could do—and do it better.

The letter was interesting and well written. George Madden, editor of the *Dispatch*, thought it had a fresh point of view. He invited Elizabeth to come and see him.

Elizabeth's heart was pounding with excitement when she went to the newspaper office. She was a pretty girl, about five feet five inches tall, with brown hair and brown eyes.

When she reached the newspaper office, a boy took her to Madden's desk. Madden was a tall, friendly-looking man, and Elizabeth felt at ease immediately.

"You write well," Madden said. "I thought you were much older than you are."

"My age has nothing to do with my ability to

write," Elizabeth said. "And neither does the fact that I'm a girl. I want to be a reporter on your newspaper."

"We've never had a woman reporter before," Madden pointed out.

"There has to be a first time," Elizabeth argued.

Madden thought for a moment. "I'll try you out," he said. "Write a story about the things that interest girls. If I like it, I'll give you a job."

When Elizabeth's story arrived at Madden's office a few days later, he was pleased with it. He sent for Elizabeth and told her that she was the *Dispatch's* newest reporter.

"Thank you, Mr. Madden," Elizabeth said. "I'm going to be a good reporter."

"I believe you," Madden said. "But there's one thing that worries me. I don't think Elizabeth Cochrane is a good name for a reporter. Sometimes I might want to use your name in headlines. Elizabeth Cochrane is too long."

"It's the only name I have," Elizabeth said with a smile, "except Pinky."

Madden laughed. "I don't think 'Pinky Cochrane' would be much better." Just then a boy walked through the office, whistling a tune by Stephen Foster.

"I've got it!" Madden cried. "Nellie Bly!" That

was the name of the song the boy was whistling. "How do you like that, Elizabeth? I mean Nellie?"

"Nellie Bly," Elizabeth said. "Nellie Bly. I like it. I'll be able to write it in half the time it takes to sign my real name."

"That will be a big advantage," Madden said with a grin, "when you become famous and have to sign your autograph."

The new Nellie Bly went to work at once. Madden encouraged her to write stories about the way people in Pittsburgh lived.

Nellie knew that there were thousands of people in Pittsburgh who had just come from Europe. Most of them were very poor and could not speak English well. They took any work they could get.

Some of the factory owners in Pittsburgh took advantage of these poor people. They made them work long hours for less than a dollar a day.

Nellie wanted to help these people. If she wrote about them, maybe the factory owners would be forced to improve their working conditions.

With her notebook in her hand, Nellie made a tour of a bottling factory. She was shocked to learn that young girls at the factory had to work fourteen hours a day. The factory was freezing cold, and many girls got sick as a result. Some of them were mere children.

Nellie wrote a sympathetic story about these girls who were overworked and underpaid. George Madden liked it.

When the owner of the bottling factory read the story, he was angry. However, that didn't stop Nellie. She wrote stories about the working conditions in other places. Sometimes she disguised herself as a poor, ignorant girl and got a job as a factory worker. She felt that she could not get the facts if the factory owners knew she was a reporter. They would try hard to hide the truth from her.

Nellie was treated exactly like the other girls. The work was hard for Nellie, but she got the truth.

Everybody liked Nellie's stories except the factory owners. Some of them stopped advertising in the *Dispatch*.

One day Madden called Nellie to his desk. "You're a good reporter, Nellie," he said. "But you have made some of our advertisers angry."

"I am trying to help the poor people of Pittsburgh," Nellie said. "I don't care about the advertisers."

"You're a reformer at heart, Nellie," Madden said. "And I'm all for you. But the *Dispatch* must have advertisers. That's where our money comes from. If we don't make enough money, we can't publish the paper."

Madden told Nellie that he was going to make her the newspaper's society editor.

"I don't think I'm going to like that," Nellie said. "But I'll try it."

In her new job Nellie spent most of her time writing about weddings, parties, and ladies' fashions. Nellie found the work dull. One day she told Madden she wanted to leave the *Dispatch*.

"I'm sorry to see you go, Nellie," Madden said. "What are you going to do?"

"My mother and I are taking a trip to Mexico," Nellie said. "That will give me a chance to think about what I want to do."

"Write some good stories about Mexico and mail them to me," Madden said. "I'll send you a check for each one we publish."

Nellie Goes to New York

Nellie traveled all over Mexico making notes about everything she saw and did. She wrote stories about the Mexican people, the food, and the flowers, and sent them to the *Dispatch*. George Madden sent her a check for each one.

Once a Mexican friend invited Nellie to go to a bullfight. She didn't want to go, but she felt that a reporter should be willing to see anything.

As Nellie sat in the arena, a trumpet sounded, and the bullfighters paraded around the ring. They were dressed in satin suits decorated with gold and silver. The bullfighters waved their hats at the crowd.

Another trumpet sounded. The people around Nellie leaped to their feet and shouted, *"El toro!"* which means "the bull" in Spanish.

As the animal entered the ring, Nellie saw that he had been driven to fury by an iron spike stuck deep into his shoulder. With a snort of rage he pawed the ground, lowered his horns, and charged at one of the bullfighters.

In one hand the bullfighter carried several barbed sticks decorated with paper streamers. In the other hand he carried a red cape. He used the cape to tease the angry bull.

Time and again the enraged animal rammed his horns into the cape while the bullfighter stepped quickly aside. As he did, he stuck one of the barbed sticks into the bull's back.

Finally the bullfighter drew his sword and drove it deep into the animal's heart.

"Poor beast!" Nellie cried as the bull fell to the ground. Turning to her Mexican friend, she said, "Bullfighting is a cruel sport."

"It's no worse than your prizefights," the Mexican

argued. "People in the United States pay to see boxers pound each other almost to death."

"I think prizefights are cruel too," Nellie said. "But bullfights are worse."

Nellie wrote a long story about the bullfight and sent it to the *Dispatch*.

After six months in Mexico, she and her mother returned to Pittsburgh. Nellie found it hard to settle down. Now that she'd had a taste of travel and adventure, she longed for more.

"I want to go to New York," she told her mother.

"What will you do there?" Mrs. Cochrane asked.

"I'll get a job on a big newspaper," Nellie said. "I can make more money in New York. Just think of the stories I can write in America's biggest city!"

Nellie wanted to get a job on *The World*, one of New York's better newspapers. She liked *The World* because it always fought for the rights of poor people. Joseph Pulitzer owned the paper. When Pulitzer came to America as a young man, he had been poor. He made a fortune in the newspaper business.

Soon after she reached New York, Nellie went to the building where *The World* was published. Mr. Pulitzer's secretary had a desk outside of his office.

"I want to see Mr. Pulitzer," Nellie said.

The excitement of New York drew Nellie Bly to look for work as a reporter for *The World*.

"He's busy," the secretary said. "Write him a letter and ask for an appointment."

Nellie wrote several letters. None was answered. Soon most of Nellie's money was gone. If she didn't get a job quickly, she would have to go back to Pittsburgh. She decided to make one last attempt to see Pulitzer.

Just as she reached his secretary's desk, a fire alarm sounded. The secretary rushed to the window to see the fire wagon go by.

Nellie ran to Pulitzer's door, opened it, and

stepped inside. Pulitzer was sitting behind a big desk. Another man was seated nearby.

Startled, the two men looked up. Nellie took a deep breath. "I'm Nellie Bly," she began. "I've come to—"

"Who let you in?" Pulitzer asked with a growl.

"I let myself in," Nellie said, flashing a smile. "Thanks to the fire, there's no one guarding your door."

"Well," Pulitzer said, melting under Nellie's smile, "as long as you're here, you might as well sit down." He turned to the other man and said, "Miss Bly, this is *The World*'s managing editor, Colonel John Cockerill."

Nellie told the two men that she wanted to work for *The World*. She showed them clippings of her stories which had been in the *Pittsburgh Dispatch*. They liked her writing style.

"What do you want to do for *The World?*" Pulitzer asked.

"Everything and anything," Nellie said earnestly.

"We might have an assignment for you," Pulitzer said. "We want to investigate New York's hospital for the poor who are mentally ill. We have heard that the hospital is a disgrace to the city."

Cockerill spoke up. "We have sent reporters to the hospital, but the doctors and nurses knew they were newspapermen. They were not allowed to see the patients and find out how they were treated."

"We have heard rumors," Pulitzer went on, "that the patients are treated cruelly. People also say that some patients at the hospital are not mentally ill. They have been sent there because they are old, tired, or poor. Their families just want to get rid of them."

"Miss Bly," Cockerill said, "if you could go to the hospital as a patient, you could find out the truth about conditions there. Are you a good enough actress to convince doctors that you are mentally sick?"

"Yes!" Nellie cried. "I know I can do it!"

"I believe her," Pulitzer said to Cockerill. "Let's give her a try."

Cockerill agreed. "If we like your work," he said to Nellie, "we will give you a permanent job."

Nellie was so happy that another big smile lit up her face.

"That smile of yours worries me," Cockerill said. "No insane person could have such a happy smile."

"I will smile no more," Nellie promised. "There's only one thing that worries me. Once I get into this hospital, how will you get me out?"

"I don't know," Cockerill admitted. "But if you can get in, we will get you out."

Blackwells Island

New York's hospital for the poor who were also mentally ill was on Blackwells Island, now called Welfare Island. It is in the East River and is part of Manhattan, a borough of New York City. Before Nellie could go to the hospital, she had to convince doctors that she was insane.

That was a problem. Nellie knew that she couldn't just go to a doctor and say that she had lost her mind. He probably wouldn't believe her. She had to convince other people that she was sick. Then they would send her to a doctor.

She went to a boardinghouse for working women and rented a room from the landlady. At dinner that night Nellie rolled her eyes, let her mouth drop open, and acted as strangely as she could. The other women looked at her nervously.

After dinner the landlady came to her and asked, "What is wrong with you? Have you some sorrow or trouble?"

"No," Nellie said, pleased that she had worried the landlady. "Why?"

"I can see it in your face," the landlady sighed. "It tells a story of great trouble."

"Yes, everything is so sad," Nellie said.

"Where are you from?" the landlady asked.

Nellie rolled her eyes again. "I do not know who I am," she said.

The landlady looked shocked. "What kind of work are you trying to get?" she asked.

"I do not know how to work," Nellie said.

"All the women who stay here work," the landlady told her.

"Do they?" Nellie asked in a whisper. "Why, they look so horrible to me, just like crazy women. I'm so afraid of them."

Alarmed, the landlady said, "We do not keep crazy women here."

"They all look crazy," Nellie went on. "There are so many crazy people about, and one can never tell what they will do." Nellie let out a loud sob that was almost a shriek. The landlady left hurriedly.

Word that Nellie was probably insane quickly spread through the boardinghouse. When Nellie went to her room, she could hear the other women talking through the thin walls.

"She's crazy all right," one of them said.

"I'm scared to death of her!" said another woman.

Shortly after dawn the next day, two policemen arrived at the house. The landlady had sent for them. They took Nellie to a nearby police station.

"Where do you come from?" a police officer asked Nellie.

"I—I do not know," Nellie replied. Fortunately she was wearing a veil so that he could not see the expression on her face.

The police officer sent her to a judge. "Come here, girl, and lift your veil," the judge said.

"To whom are you speaking?" Nellie asked.

"A girl whose face I would like to see," the judge answered. "If the queen of England were here, she would lift her veil."

"I am not the queen of England," Nellie said proudly. Still, she lifted her veil. She rolled her eyes again and let her mouth drop open.

The judge decided to send Nellie to a nearby hospital. Doctors there would examine her to see if she were mentally ill.

The doctors at the hospital asked Nellie only a few questions before deciding that she was hopelessly insane. Nellie was astonished that their examination was so brief. At that time people were only beginning to learn how to treat mental illness. Still, it was obvious these doctors had not had proper training.

Soon the news spread that there was a mysterious insane girl in the city who did not know her name. Reporters from all the New York papers, except *The World*, came to interview Nellie.

She was afraid of the reporters. She knew they

had bright, inquiring minds and that they might suspect what she was doing.

Nellie was a good actress, and she gave clever answers to the reporters' questions. However, she wanted to get rid of them quickly.

Turning to a nurse who was with her, she began to scream. "I never saw such a lot of crazy men as there are around this place," Nellie shrieked. The nurse asked the reporters to leave at once.

Soon afterward Nellie was put on a boat for Blackwells Island. When the boat landed there, and Nellie stepped ashore, a guard in uniform grabbed her arm.

"What is this place?" Nellie asked, concealing how glad she was to be there.

"This is Blackwells Island," the guard said, "a place for insane people. You'll never leave it."

Even though she knew *The World* would get her out, Nellie shuddered.

"Nellie Bly" in Headlines

Now that she had succeeded in being sent to Blackwells Island, Nellie decided to stop acting insane. She wanted to find out if the doctors and nurses would notice that a perfectly sane person was in the hospital for the mentally ill. So Nellie became her own self again, a bright and charming young woman, normal in every way.

Soon after her arrival, Nellie was examined by a doctor. "I am not sick," she told him, "and I do not want to stay here. No one has a right to shut me up in this way." The doctor paid no attention to anything she said.

Nellie realized that many other sane people might be locked up on Blackwells Island. Without friends outside, they might never escape.

After being examined by the doctor, Nellie was sent to a room full of women patients. She studied the poor, mentally ill women. Some of them were talking nonsense to invisible people. Others were crying.

"They look so lost and hopeless," Nellie said to herself. Her heart went out to them.

That night Nellie had her first meal in the hospital. It was only a cup of tea, a piece of bread, and five prunes.

Nellie tried to eat the bread. The butter on it was so old and bad that she couldn't force it down. The tea had no sugar in it and had a terrible taste.

After supper attendants forced Nellie and the other women to take baths. The water was freezing cold. Nellie's teeth chattered, and her lips turned blue.

When she finished bathing, she was given a thin

slip to sleep in. Then a nurse locked her in a tiny room and told her to go to bed.

The bed was extremely hard, and there was no heat in the room. Nellie began to shiver. She asked a nurse if she could have a flannel nightgown.

"We have no flannel gowns in this hospital," the nurse said.

"I do not like to sleep without one," Nellie pleaded.

"I don't care about that," the nurse said. "You are in a public place now, and you can't expect to get anything. This is charity. You should be thankful that you are here."

"But the city pays to keep this place up," Nellie argued. "It pays you to be kind to the poor people who are brought here."

"Well," the nurse said, "don't expect kindness here, for you won't get it."

Shivering, Nellie lay awake looking at the locked door and the barred windows. What if fire broke out? Escape would be impossible. She and the other patients would burn to death.

The next morning Nellie tried to eat her breakfast, but it was hopeless. She found a spider in her bread.

Later, when she was taken outside for exercise, Nellie walked by the kitchen where the food for the doctors and nurses was prepared. She looked in the window and saw melons, grapes, and other fruit. Fresh bread and expensive meats were on the kitchen table.

"The doctors and nurses have the best of everything," Nellie thought, "while the patients starve."

That same day Nellie almost cried when she saw the way two nurses treated a poor, helpless woman who had obviously become very ill. The woman kept saying she wanted to go home.

"Shut up!" one of the nurses snapped at the pitiful patient. The woman started screaming. The nurses slapped her face and knocked her head against the wall. The patient screamed even louder.

Nellie rushed out of the room to find a doctor. She told the doctor what the nurses had done. The doctor ignored her. Evidently cruelty was the normal way of life in this hospital, Nellie thought. She wondered how the mentally ill patients could ever hope to get well.

After she had spent ten days in the hospital, *The World* sent a lawyer to the island. He arranged for Nellie to leave. He told the doctors that Nellie's friends would pay for a private nurse.

Nellie went straight to *The World*'s office and started writing her story about the hospital. Pulitzer and Cockerill were extremely pleased with it.

"You are a good reporter," Cockerill told Nellie. "We want you to work for us permanently."

Nellie was delighted when she saw a copy of *The World* with her story on page one. The headlines read:

BEHIND ASYLUM BARS

THE MYSTERY OF THE UNKNOWN

INSANE GIRL

How Nellie Bly Deceived Judges, Reporters, and Medical Experts

Now Nellie's name was in headlines. As a result of her story, some important citizens investigated Blackwells Island. They found that Nellie had told the truth about conditions there.

New York City started spending a million dollars more each year for the care of the insane. Nellie was happy about that. "I am glad that the mentally ill will be better cared for because of my work," she said.

Nellie Smiles Again

After Nellie became a permanent reporter on *The World,* she started working for an editor named Morrill Goddard.

"I'm glad to have a young woman on my staff," he told Nellie. "I wish I'd had one long ago."

He suggested that Nellie get a job in one of New York's box factories and write a story about the poor girls who worked there.

Nellie went to several factories before she found work. "You will not be paid anything for the first two weeks," the man who hired her said. "After that we'll pay you a dollar and a half a week."

A girl named Nora took charge of Nellie and tried to teach her to make boxes. Nellie, however, spent most of her time talking to the other girls.

The World used these drawings of girls in a box factory to highlight Nellie's story.

198820

CODY MEMORIAL LIBRARY
SOUTHWESTERN UNIVERSITY
GEORGETOWN, TEXAS 78626

"How do you like the factory?" Nellie asked a young girl who had been there only a few days.

"I don't like working two weeks without pay," the girl said. "And I know that many girls are fired at the end of that time. Then the factory owners hire other girls to work two weeks for nothing."

"That's slave labor!" Nellie exclaimed angrily.

Nellie learned that many girls who worked in the factory were only sixteen years old. They made boxes ten to twelve hours a day, six days a week. Nellie was touched by their stories. One girl and her twelve-year-old brother supported their father who was too sick to work.

At the end of the day, Nellie left the factory and returned to *The World*. Her heart ached as she wrote about the poor girls who worked so hard for so little money.

The next morning Goddard stopped at Nellie's desk. "What's happened to that famous smile of yours?" he asked. "I haven't seen it much recently."

"In my work there's not much to smile about," Nellie said. "The mentally ill, the poor—" Her voice trailed off.

"Cheer up, Nellie!" Goddard said. "Life's not all that bad. But I think you need a change. I want you to write some stories with laughter in them. How would you like to go husband hunting?"

"And write about it?" Nellie asked, interested at once.

Goddard explained that there were marriage agents in New York who made money finding husbands for lonesome women and wives for lonesome men. He asked Nellie to visit one of these agents and pose as a woman who wanted a husband. "It should make a funny story," Goddard said.

"All right," Nellie agreed. "Just so I don't have to get married in order to get the story. That might be funny to you, but not to me."

Nellie went to a marriage agent and told him she was looking for a husband. The agent seemed surprised that such a pretty girl needed his help.

"I should think you would have plenty of friends," the agent said.

"The men I meet are so dull," Nellie explained. "I thought I might find a better husband here."

The agent seemed pleased. He asked Nellie to fill out a form describing herself and giving her name and address.

Nellie could not give her real name, or the agent would know she was a reporter. "My name is Gypsy Hastings," she said, "and I live with an aunt. I can't give you my address because my aunt is terribly strict. She would punish me if she found out that I had been to a marriage agent."

The man let Nellie fill out the form without giving her address. He told her she would have to pay him five dollars before he would introduce her to any men.

"If I find you a husband," the agent said, "you will have to pay me $100."

Nellie rented a post office box under the name of Gypsy Hastings. She told the agent to write to her there. Soon she had a letter asking her to come to the agency and meet a fine gentleman.

When Nellie arrived, the agent introduced her to a tall man who had brown hair and a mustache.

"I am the president of two mining companies," the man said, "and I can play many musical instruments. I was a child prodigy. People used to come from miles around to hear me. When I was eight years old, I could speak and write Latin, and when I was ten, I wrote Greek. I was always awfully smart. I am well known as a writer and—"

Nellie could hardly keep a straight face. She had to remind herself that a good story depended on her self-control.

"How lovely to be a writer," Nellie said. "What do you write for? Those horrid newspapers?"

"I write for magazines," the man said. "I also go to many parties and am very popular with the ladies. They like me so much that—"

This picture of Nellie Bly shows the good looks and high spirits that won her fame and fortune.

The minutes dragged into hours. "He's a regular talking machine," Nellie thought. Finally she could stand it no longer.

"It's time for me to go home," she announced.

"May I see you again?" the man asked.

Under her breath Nellie murmured, "Not so long as oatmeal is cheap." Then aloud she said, "I can't see you again. My aunt is so strict." Nellie fled.

Later the agent introduced her to other men who were looking for wives. One asked, "Can you cook and sweep well? Can you make beds? Are you a good washer and ironer?"

Nellie smiled when she remembered that one reason she had become a reporter was to escape such chores.

"You don't want a wife," she told the man. "You want a slave."

Nellie asked another man what he thought of the women he had met through the agent.

"With one exception they have been perfectly horrible," the man said.

"In what way?" Nellie asked.

"Every way. I never wanted to see them again."

"You must be hard to please," Nellie said.

"Don't think that," the man protested. "If I had only met someone like you before, I would—"

"I must go," Nellie interrupted. "My aunt is so strict."

Nellie wrote a long, funny story about her experiences as a husband hunter. The last line was, "I am still in search of a husband, and the agent still has my five dollars."

"This is great, Nellie," Goddard said when he had read her story. "You certainly are lucky to have such a strict aunt."

Nellie laughed happily. She began to think up ideas for other stories that would make people laugh. She went to a ballet school, took lessons, and told what a hard time she had learning how to dance.

Then she went to a theater and applied for a job as a chorus girl. Nellie decided that the manager wasn't very particular for he hired her right away.

The first time Nellie went on the stage, she got all mixed up. When the girls kicked one way, Nellie kicked the other. The audience howled with laughter. As the other girls danced toward the front of the stage, Nellie danced toward the back. When she corrected herself and ran to the front, the other girls danced to the rear.

Right after the curtain went down, the manager fired her. Nellie didn't mind. She wrote a funny story about her debut on the stage.

"I had much rather be a reporter than a dancer," she said.

"Good Duck, Nellie!"

Nellie had always liked travel stories. One of her favorites was *Around the World in Eighty Days*, written by a Frenchman, Jules Verne, in 1872.

In the book a man bets a great deal of money that he can go around the world in 80 days. The few people who went around the world at that time usually took a year or more. There were no airplanes or automobiles then.

Although Verne's hero, Phileas Fogg, wins his bet with just one second to spare, most people who read the book thought such a speedy trip was impossible. Nellie, however, believed that she could go around the world in less than 80 days.

She decided to try to get the editors of *The World* to pay for her trip. Nellie knew the journey would cost a great deal of money, but she thought the newspaper would profit by it. Thousands of people would buy *The World* to read about her adventures.

"A newspaper named *The World* ought to send a reporter around the world," Nellie told the editors.

"That makes sense," one of them said, "but if anyone goes, it will be a man—not a helpless girl."

"I'm not helpless," Nellie said, tossing her head.

"It would be easier for a man," one of the editors argued.

"Very well," Nellie said. "If you send a man, I'll start the same day for another newspaper and beat him."

The editors were afraid Nellie would do just that. They agreed to let her go.

Nellie decided not to take many clothes. Too much baggage might delay her. She took just one dress and one blouse, and carried a small bag.

On November 14, 1889, Nellie sailed for England

from Jersey City, just across the Hudson River from New York.

"I'm off," she said as the ship inched away from the dock. "And I'll be back in less than 80 days." If Nellie had doubts, she didn't show them.

Her ship reached England in seven days. There Nellie found a message from Jules Verne asking her to visit him in France. She couldn't spare much time, but she wanted to see him. If he hadn't written his famous book, she wouldn't be racing around the world.

Nellie stopped to see the Vernes on her way to Italy. *"Mon Dieu!"* the Frenchman said when he met her. "What a child! Is it possible that a baby is going all that long way alone?"

Madame Verne turned to her husband and said, "She is trim and strong. I believe, Jules, that she will make your hero look foolish. She will beat your record."

Nellie smiled with delight.

Jules Verne didn't speak very good English, but he tried. As Nellie got ready to go, he asked, "How does one say in English *'bonne chance'*? Good duck? Very well, good duck, Nellie."

Nellie burst out laughing, but Verne didn't mind. "Oh, it's good luck, not good duck," he said. "Well, no matter, the feeling is the same in any case."

After leaving the Vernes, Nellie took a train for a seaport in Italy. There she boarded a ship named the *Victoria* for the next stage of her journey.

Nellie wanted to send a story about her latest adventures to *The World*. "Do I have time to go to the telegraph office before the ship sails?" she asked a fellow passenger.

"You'll have time if you hurry," he said. "I know where the telegraph office is. I'll go with you."

Nellie wrote a long story about her trip through France and Italy. Then she asked the telegraph operator to send it to New York.

The man who had come with her tugged at her sleeve. "Hurry!" he said. "I didn't know it would take so long to send a telegram. We may miss our ship."

"No!" Nellie cried in dismay.

"Can you run?" her companion asked.

"Like lightning," Nellie said.

The man grabbed her hand, and they dashed through the streets. When Nellie heard a ship's whistle, she felt sure it meant the *Victoria* had sailed without her.

Still, she and her friend raced on. After turning a sharp corner, they came to the dock and saw that the ship was still there. Nellie said a prayer of thanks.

Nellie's checkered coat became almost as well known as Nellie herself. She traveled with only the clothes she could carry in one bag.

Bad News for Nellie

The *Victoria* sailed calmly across the Mediterranean Sea, through the Suez Canal, and into the Red Sea. At one port several Arab boys begged Nellie to throw some coins into the water.

Nellie tossed a dime into the sea. One of the Arab boys dived after it. In a few seconds he came up, smiling at Nellie, with the silver coin shining between his lips.

When Nellie reached Ceylon, an island off the coast of India, she found that she would have to wait five days for a ship bound for Hong Kong. From Hong Kong, just off the coast of China, she was supposed to sail for America on the *Oceanic* on December 28.

Nellie was worried. If she missed the *Oceanic*, she had no chance to get back to New York in less than 80 days.

Still, there was nothing she could do about it now. So she decided to enjoy her stay in Ceylon. She rode all over the island in a rickshaw—a little cart pulled by two men—seeing the sights.

Nellie was interested in the snake charmers of Ceylon. One near her hotel asked if she would like to see a snake dance. Nellie gave him some money.

The man lifted the lid of a little basket that he

carried, and a deadly cobra crawled out and curled up on the ground. While waving a red cloth at the snake, the man started playing on a fife.

The angry cobra rose up and struck at the cloth with his fangs. As the man raised the cloth higher, the snake rose until it was standing on its tail.

Nellie was horrified when the snake lashed out at the snake charmer. The man, however, was too quick for the cobra. He caught the snake by the head and put it back in the basket.

Sight-seeing was fun, but Nellie was glad when her ship, the *Oriental*, finally sailed for Hong Kong. If the ship went fast enough, there was still a chance that she could catch the *Oceanic*.

The morning after leaving Ceylon, a loud knock on the door of the next cabin awakened Nellie. She knew that several small children and a nurse occupied that cabin.

"What does baby say to papa?" she heard the children's father ask. "Come now, what does baby say to papa?"

Nellie heard a shrill voice cry from inside the children's cabin, "Papa!"

"And what does the moo cow say, baby?"

The baby didn't answer. "What does the moo cow say?" the man asked again. "Tell papa what the moo cow says."

When the baby still didn't answer, Nellie decided she could stand it no longer. "For heavens sake, baby!" she shouted through the wall. "Tell papa what the moo cow says so I can get some sleep."

Nellie often found it hard to sleep because she worried about missing the *Oceanic*. The *Oriental* seemed so slow.

On the way to Hong Kong, the ship stopped at Singapore where Nellie went sight-seeing and shopping.

In one store she saw a tiny monkey and fell in love with it. "Will the monkey bite?" she asked the storekeeper.

"No," he replied. "This is a good monkey."

Nellie bought it. "Now I won't be traveling alone anymore," she said.

After leaving Singapore, Nellie's ship picked up speed. She was excited when it docked at Hong Kong ahead of schedule. The *Oceanic* was still there. "Now I'm sure I can circle the world in less than 80 days," she told herself.

Bad news awaited Nellie in Hong Kong, however. The day after she had left New York, another girl had started racing around the world.

That girl's name was Elizabeth Bisland, and a magazine was paying for her trip. Miss Bisland had recently passed through Hong Kong going in the opposite direction from Nellie. She had told everyone that she was going to beat Nellie back to New York.

Nellie was almost sick with worry. She would feel terrible if Miss Bisland reached New York before she did.

72 Days, 6 Hours, 11 Minutes!

Soon after leaving Hong Kong, the *Oceanic* stopped in Japan to pick up passengers and mail. There Nellie saw copies of *The World* for the first time since leaving home.

She read that her newspaper was having a Nellie Bly Guessing Game. The person who came closest to guessing how long it would take Nellie to go around the world would win a free trip to Europe.

The World also printed some poems that readers had written about Nellie. She liked one that said:

Around the world goes Nellie Bly
Like a swallow on the fly.

Yet Nellie traveled more like a turtle than a swallow. After the *Oceanic* left Japan, it ran into stormy weather and just poked along.

Some people thought that Nellie's monkey was bad luck. They wanted to throw it overboard. Nellie wouldn't think of that.

She was, however, worried about the ship's speed. Would Miss Bisland beat her around the world? Nellie could think of nothing else.

Finally she went to see the ship's captain. "I had rather return to New York dead and on time, than alive and late," she told him. The captain promised to go faster. Signs posted on the ship's bulletin board read:

We'll win or die
For Nellie Bly!

When the *Oceanic* increased its speed, Nellie cheered up. She thanked the captain and the crew when the ship reached San Francisco on time.

With her monkey sitting on her shoulder, Nellie boarded a special train for the final dash across America. Crowds gathered in every town and city along the way to see Nellie Bly go by.

On January 25, 1890, the train reached Jersey City, where she had left 72 days, 6 hours, and 11 minutes earlier. She had beaten the record of Jules Verne's hero by almost eight days. Elizabeth Bisland was still somewhere on the Atlantic. Nellie had won!

An enormous crowd was waiting to greet Nellie. As she stepped off the train, she flung her cap into the air with joy. The crowd roared.

Across the river in New York City, cannon were fired in honor of her victory. Then each ship in the river blew its whistle.

Nellie and her monkey were taken across the river by boat and then driven to the newspaper office. Thousands of people surrounded *The World* building.

"Hurrah for Nellie Bly!" they shouted as the young reporter drove up in a carriage.

The editors of *The World* congratulated her on

This cartoon, appearing on the day of her return, shows Nellie in the company of other famous world travelers in history and fiction.

her triumph. That day nearly all the front page was devoted to her trip.

Newspapers all over America and in most other countries printed stories about Nellie. She was now the most famous young woman on earth. Everybody wanted her autograph.

"Thank goodness my name is now Nellie Bly," she said. "I'd never have time to write Elizabeth Cochrane for all these people."

Messages of congratulation came to Nellie from all parts of the earth. The one she liked best was from Jules Verne. "Bravo! Bravo! Bravo!" it said.

Nellie was glad to be in America again and back in her apartment. She put her monkey in the living room in a cage, but the little animal didn't like being locked up.

The next morning it looked at Nellie with such sad eyes that she opened the door and let it out. The little animal ran into the kitchen and hopped up on a shelf where Nellie kept her best dishes and glasses. It started throwing the dishes on the floor. Before Nellie could catch her pet, it had smashed the glasses too.

"You little rascal!" Nellie said. "I'm afraid you don't like living in an apartment."

The next day Nellie gave the monkey to a zoo. She hated to part with her pet, but she knew it would be happier there. "And I'll save money on dishes," she said.

Still, Nellie didn't really have to worry about money. She was now one of the highest paid reporters in America.

Before going back to work for *The World*, she went on a lecture tour. People all over America wanted to see her and hear her speak.

Nellie's lectures helped make world travel popular. From her, people learned how easy and safe it was to go to faraway places. People from different countries got to know one another better and became friendly.

Indirectly, Nellie did a great deal for world peace and understanding.

Around the World Again

Soon after Nellie returned to *The World*, America was hit by a business depression. Millions of people lost their jobs. Other millions had their wages cut.

One day Nellie's editor called her to his office. "The workers at the Pullman Company have walked off their jobs," he told her. "They are on strike for better working conditions."

"I have heard that the Pullman workers have nothing to strike about," Nellie said.

"I want the truth," the editor said. "I want you to talk to the strikers and write stories about them."

The Pullman Company, which made railroad sleeping cars, was located in the town of Pullman, a suburb of Chicago, Illinois. On her way to Pullman, Nellie stopped in Chicago. The newspapers were full of stories about the strike. They said the strikers were rioting and burning their houses.

People in Chicago advised Nellie not to go to Pullman. "You might get killed," they said. Yet Nellie was determined to get her story.

She was astonished when she reached Pullman. There was no rioting or burning.

"These are the only homes we have," a striker told Nellie. "Why would we burn them down?"

Nellie went all over the town talking to people. She learned that the Pullman Company made the workers live in Pullman. The company owned all the houses and made the workers pay high rents.

The workers thought that when their wages were cut, the rents should be cut too. "We must have either higher wages or lower rents," one man told Nellie.

She found that many children did not have enough to eat. There was no money for clothes or shoes. The Pullman Company even made them pay to take books out of the library.

Nellie quickly changed her mind about the workers having nothing to strike about. She wrote stories favorable to them. Many people who read Nellie's stories also changed their minds about the strike.

One person who had always sided with the strikers was John Peter Altgeld, the governor of Illinois. Nellie wanted to interview him. Someone told her that he hated reporters.

Nellie trembled when she rang the bell at the governor's house. A servant took her to his office.

After answering Nellie's questions, the governor asked her what she had seen in the town of Pullman. She told him about the poor people she had described in her stories.

"Were your stories published in *The World?*" the governor asked.

"Why, certainly!" Nellie exclaimed. "*The World* hires reporters to find out the truth about everything."

"Then I'm going to start reading *The World*," the governor said.

As Nellie got ready to leave, she smiled and said, "I was dreadfully afraid of you. I was told you hated reporters."

"So I do," Governor Altgeld admitted. "But it was your smile that made me welcome you. Your smile is worth a million dollars."

"Oh!" Nellie gasped. "How I wish I could sell it!"

The governor laughed. "You keep it," he said. "You can get anything you want with that smile."

Perhaps Governor Altgeld was right about Nellie's smile being worth a million dollars. For not long afterward she met a millionaire named Robert J. Seaman. Nellie and her smile charmed him, and he asked her to marry him.

"You won't need to work after you're married to me," Seaman said.

"I like my work," Nellie said. "But I like you even better."

After the wedding the Seamans took a long, slow trip around the world. This time Nellie didn't have to worry about catching trains or ships.

The Seamans were very happy, but not many years after the wedding, Robert Seaman died of a heart attack. Nellie tried to run his business, but she was not a good businesswoman. She lost a great deal of money.

When Nellie was nearly fifty years old, she became a reporter again. She worked on the *New York Evening Journal.*

Nellie was pleased to find that there were so many young newspaperwomen in New York now. She had lunch with half a dozen of them one day and talked about her early days with *The World.*

"There were very few women reporters then," Nellie said, glancing around the table. "Now look!" "You were a pioneer," one of the girls said. "You proved that women reporters are just as good as men. You made it easy for us to get newspaper jobs."

Nellie smiled, pleased that she had been able to help them.

Until she died in 1922, Nellie worked for *The Journal*. She had enjoyed every minute of her career as a reporter. People everywhere had admired her stories for their honesty and wit.

In the story about her death, *The Journal* called her "the best reporter in America."

Ladies of the Press—at Work!

Nellie Bly's daring—and her outstanding ability as a reporter—opened the door just a crack to other women reporters. It was pushed open a bit wider by other bold women who followed Nellie. One of these was Winifred Black, who braved the dangers of flooded Galveston, Texas, in 1900 to send word about the city to the readers of the New York *Journal.* Another was the fearless Rheta Childe Dorr, who covered the Russian Revolution in 1917 for the New York *Daily Mail.* Her news reports were sent from her post in the field with a company of Russian women soldiers.

These reporters wore frilly shirtwaists and petticoats. They lived at a time when women who worked in any job other than teaching were thought to be unladylike. Still, they had made up their minds to be reporters—and to do their work well!

Today, women work on newspapers and in the, newsrooms of radio and television stations all over the United States. More and more women reporters are becoming well known to newspaper readers and television viewers as good all-around reporters as well as reporters of "women's news." They cover foreign, political, and local news. They even cover news from the battlefronts of the world. A few of these ladies of the press—of the recent past and present—are shown in the pages that follow.

Barbara Walters   Melba Tolliver

BARBARA WALTERS became a familiar figure to the television viewing public as the cohost of NBC television's "Today" show.
After working several years behind the scenes writing, pro-
ducing, and filming public-affairs programs for CBS, Barbara
was hired as a writer for NBC's "Today." In 1965 Barbara
was given a chance to try out as cohost and passed the test
with flying colors. On the "Today" show she became widely
known for her exciting feature stories and for her interviews
with the great and the near-great. She is seen above inter-
viewing President Richard M. Nixon.

MELBA TOLLIVER, ABC television's on-the-air newswoman, moved
from a secretary's desk at ABC to the network's newsroom
after a series of lucky breaks. Hard work in a year-long program of study and on her New York City newsbeat kept her
there! Television audiences welcomed the addition of capable
Melba Tolliver to the all-male staff of ABC's "Eyewitness
News."

55

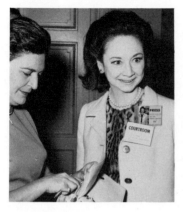 

Dorothy Kilgallen   Pauline Frederick

DOROTHY KILGALLEN found a job as a newspaper reporter in the summer of 1931, following her freshman year in college. Dorothy had such an exciting summer as a cub reporter that she never went back to school! Over the years she became America's best-known woman reporter, covering disasters, political events, and some of the most sensational criminal trials of the day. Dorothy Kilgallen was a columnist and a radio and television star, as well as a working reporter until her death in 1965. She is seen above being searched as she enters a courtroom to cover a big story.

PAULINE FREDERICK's first big opportunity came in 1948 when, as an ABC television reporter, she was sent to cover a foreign ministers' meeting. She did such a fine job that she was excused from covering "women's news" and given her own newsbeat. Five years later she moved to NBC, where she became a correspondent at the United Nations. Pauline Frederick has had a long career as a reporter covering exciting events in national and international news. But the most challenging beat of all has been the United Nations.

Marguerite Higgins   Doris Fleeson

MARGUERITE HIGGINS was always sure that she would become a foreign correspondent. When Maggie was twenty-five years old, she persuaded the New York *Herald Tribune* to send her to Paris. While she was in Europe, she covered the advance of American soldiers into Germany during the last months of World War II. In the Korean War she faced death daily with troops in the field. When war broke out in Vietnam, Maggie was ready once more. She died a soldier's death in 1965 from a rare disease which she had contracted in Vietnam. She is seen above on a transport plane in Korea.

DORIS FLEESON was best known as a hard-hitting political reporter. She learned her business as a reporter on the New York *Daily News* and then moved to Washington, D.C., where, with her husband, she wrote a column called "Capitol Stuff." She left the *News* during World War II to cover the war for a women's magazine. She was best known in recent years for her syndicated column on political affairs, which appeared in 190 newspapers at the time of her death in 1970. She is seen above at the front in World War II.

57

ANNIE OAKLEY
1860–1926

stumbled into a "man's job" in 1875
when she challenged expert marksman Frank Butler to a shooting
match. The pretty girl from Darke
County, Ohio, won the match and a
husband too! After Annie and Frank
were married, Annie became part of
her husband's act. Audiences cheered
wildly for the girl who had proved
that she could outshoot any man, and
Annie soon became the star of the
act. As a leading attraction in Buffalo
Bill's Wild West Show, Annie's feats
thrilled her fans in America and
Europe. The tiny "lady wing shot"
became the adopted daughter of
Chief Sitting Bull, the friend of kings
and queens, and the darling of
audiences everywhere. A terrible
accident almost ended her career,
but Annie fought her way back
to health and proved once again
that she was the finest marksman
of her day.

Annie Oakley
The Shooting Star

by Charles P. Graves

Copyright © 1961 by Charles P. Graves

Thanksgiving Turkey

"Please let me shoot your gun, father," Phoebe Anne Moses begged.

It was the day before Thanksgiving. Annie had followed her stepfather into the forest. "If I ask him often enough," Annie thought, "he'll let me shoot."

"Annie," her stepfather said, "shooting is a man's job."

"Women used guns to protect themselves from Indian attacks right here in Ohio," Annie said. "They had to when the men were away hunting. Lydia told me. She learned about it in school." Lydia was Annie's oldest sister.

Of course there were no Indians roaming about Ohio now. The year was 1867.

"All right, Annie," her stepfather agreed. "You win! You can shoot at the next game bird we see. When you miss," he laughed, "I'll try to hit it."

Annie's real father, Jacob Moses, had died when Annie was five. Her stepfather was named Dan Brumbaugh. He was a good man. But he did not think that a girl belonged behind a gun. So he decided to play a trick on Annie. He felt sure the trick would cure her of wanting to shoot.

He put some extra powder in his gun. He knew this would make it kick extra hard. Of course he did not want to hurt Annie. But he did want to make her afraid of a gun.

Suddenly they heard the "gobble, gobble" of a wild turkey. The big bird was just flying from the branch of a tree.

"Now's your chance, Annie," her stepfather said, handing her the gun.

Annie aimed carefully. When it felt right, she pulled the trigger.

"Ouch!" cried Annie as the gun roared. The butt of the gun slammed into Annie's face and shoulder. The kick was much worse than her stepfather thought it would be.

"Oh, Annie, dear, I'm sorry," her stepfather cried. "I didn't mean to hurt you. I just meant to scare you a little."

Annie held back her tears. "I'm not sorry," she said. "I'm glad. Just look! We'll have turkey for Thanksgiving!"

Annie pointed to the wild bird that was lying on the ground. She had shot it neatly in the head.

Her stepfather put his arm around her. "You're a good shot, Annie. I'm proud of you."

Annie Oakley spent her childhood in a log cabin
much like this one.

Together they walked home through the forest.
Soon they reached the log cabin where they lived.
Annie's mother met them at the door.

Mr. Brumbaugh held the turkey up for her to see.
"Annie shot it," he said.

"How did you do it, Annie?" her mother asked.

"It was easy, mother," Annie said. "When it felt
right, I just pulled the trigger."

For the rest of her life, shooting would be easy
for Annie. She was on her way to becoming a shooting star.

Off to Work

The country near Greenville, Ohio, where Annie lived, was beautiful and wild. Annie loved to walk barefoot through the woods and fields, gathering nuts and berries. In the spring she climbed dogwood trees and picked the white flowers to put in her hair.

But Annie did not have much time for play. She helped her mother with the housework. And she helped take care of Johnny and Hulda, her little brother and sister. Sometimes she fed the baby, Emily.

It was a busy and happy life. Sometimes Annie and Johnny built bird traps out of cornstalks. The birds they caught were good to eat.

But one day Annie's stepfather became sick. After a short time he died. It was a sad day for Annie and her family.

Annie's mother had very little money to buy food for her seven children. She got a job as a nurse, but it did not pay much. There was no one to take care of the children while she worked. So she sent the younger ones to stay with friends.

Annie went to live with Mr. and Mrs. Crawford Eddington. They had a home for orphans—children whose mothers and fathers had died. Mrs. Eddington taught Annie to sew. Annie often mended the children's clothes. And she helped in other ways. Mrs. Eddington wanted to pay Annie for her work. But she did not have enough money.

One day a well-to-do farmer came to the home. He asked to speak to Mrs. Eddington. Annie showed him into the living room. Then she called Mrs. Eddington.

Annie left them in the room, but she stood close by the door outside. She knew she should not listen to their conversation, but Annie had more curiosity than ten kittens.

"I'm looking for a girl to live with my family," the farmer told Mrs. Eddington. "I will pay her 50 cents a week. She won't have much work to do, and she can go to school."

Annie ran into the room. "Let me have the job," she cried. "I'll work hard."

"This is Annie Moses," Mrs. Eddington told the farmer. "She's small, but she's a hard worker. I'm sure that she will suit you."

"I'll pay you 50 cents each week," the farmer said.

"I don't want you to give me the money," Annie cried. "My mother needs it very much. Please send it to her."

The farmer agreed, and Annie was soon ready to leave.

Escape

Annie rode in a wagon to the farmer's house. The farmer's wife met her at the front gate.

"I'd hoped we were going to get a bigger girl," she said to Annie. "You're going to have to work mighty hard."

"I'm willing to work hard," Annie said, standing on her toes so she would look taller. But Annie did not know what the woman meant by hard work.

The farmer's wife made Annie get up at four o'clock. First, Annie had to milk the cows and feed the pigs and chickens. Then she had to build a fire in the stove and cook breakfast. Next, Annie pumped water, washed the dishes, and dressed the baby. Then the woman made her sweep the house and scrub the kitchen floor. Annie never had any time to rest or play. And the farmer's wife would not let her go to school.

However, Annie did learn to ride a horse. She rode horseback when she brought the cows in from the fields to the barn. The only reason the farmer let Annie ride was because it saved time. That meant more time for her to do other chores.

On horseback Annie made a pretty picture. Her lovely brown hair flew in the wind.

"Riding is a lot of fun," Annie thought.

But that was all the fun Annie had. The farmer's wife scolded her many times a day.

Sometimes Annie was so tired that she almost fell asleep while working. Then she remembered that the farmer was sending money to her mother.

"I must stay awake," Annie said to herself. "Mother needs the money."

One night Annie heard the farmer talking to his wife.

"Annie is the biggest bargain we've ever had," he said.

"Aren't you sending money to her mother?" his wife asked.

"Of course not," Annie heard the farmer say. "Annie just thinks that I'm sending it. I wrote to her mother and said I could not pay Annie any money. But I told her that Annie is happy with us and is going to school. Her mother wrote back. She said Annie could stay."

"You're a smart man," the farmer's wife said with a sly grin. "We must not let Annie know her mother isn't getting any money."

Annie was angry. To think that she had worked so hard for nothing! She was afraid to say anything to the farmer or his wife. They would probably treat her even worse. And they might never let her go home.

That night, when Annie went to bed, she started to cry. But she soon fought back the tears.

"I must not cry," she thought. "I must plan to escape." Before she went to sleep, Annie had made a plan.

The next night Annie went to bed with all her clothes on. She lay there quietly until she heard the farmer and his wife go to bed. Soon she heard loud snoring from their room. Annie got up. She stuffed her pillow and an old blanket under the bed covers. If the farmer's wife looked in the room, she would think Annie was asleep in bed.

Annie tied her few belongings into a bundle. She started to tiptoe down the stairs. A loose board creaked loudly.

"What was that?" Annie heard the farmer's wife ask. "What was that noise?"

Annie froze in her tracks. Her heart seemed to beat as loudly as a drum. Surely they would hear it.

"That was a mouse," the farmer said to his wife. "Go back to sleep."

Annie could not help smiling. "I'm a pretty big mouse," she thought. "Now I must be quiet as a mouse."

She waited for the farmer and his wife to go back to sleep. Then she crept down the stairs and out of the house. When she reached the road, she started to run. There was a railroad station nearby. Annie planned to take the first train, no matter where it went.

Luckily the first train went to a place near Annie's home. She climbed aboard.

"They can't catch me now," she said to herself. "I'll be home soon."

Quail for Sale

Annie was glad to see her mother. And her mother was really happy to see Annie. After they stopped hugging, Annie's mother told her some good news. She had just married again.

Annie's new stepfather was named Joseph Shaw. He was quite old. So the children called him "Grandpap Shaw." They loved him very much.

Grandpap Shaw bought a farm for Annie's mother and her children. He built a nice house for them. But he had to borrow money from the bank to pay for it.

It was hard for Mr. Shaw to earn enough money to pay the bank back. Annie wanted to help. So she started hunting again. She often shot birds, rabbits, and squirrels for her family to eat. Her mother did not have to buy any meat. This saved money which could be used to help pay for the house.

Annie bought her shotgun shells from the general store in Greenville. It was run by Mr. Charles Katzenberger. One day Annie brought a present to Mr. Katzenberger. The present was six fat birds, called quail. Annie knew that Mr. Katzenberger liked to eat quail.

"Thank you, Annie," Mr. Katzenberger said. "You are a thoughtful girl. And, my," he cried, looking closely at the quail, "you're a mighty good shot."

"I try to hit them in the head," Annie said proudly. "That way no lead shots get in the meat. You could break a tooth if you bit into a shot."

"That's right," Mr. Katzenberger agreed. "And that gives me an idea. I know a man who runs a hotel. He likes to serve quail in his dining room. He will pay good money for your quail."

"That's wonderful!" Annie cried. "I can shoot all the quail he can use. The money will help pay off the bank loan."

Every week Annie brought quail to Mr. Katzenberger. He sent them to a hotel in Cincinnati. Because her quail were shot cleanly through the head, Annie got a big price. The hotel owner knew that his guests would not break their teeth on Annie's birds.

Annie gave most of the money she made to Grandpap Shaw. He paid it to the bank. One day Grandpap Shaw came home from the bank and called Annie. "I made the last payment today," he said happily. "This house is now ours. Perhaps I should say that it's yours, Annie."

"Oh, no!" Annie cried. "*Ours* is the right word. We all own this house together."

Annie did not know it then, but she was not going to live in the house very long.

A few days later she had a letter from her oldest sister, Lydia. Lydia was now married to a man named Joe Stein. They lived in Cincinnati. Lydia asked Annie to come for a visit.

Annie shot quail for a few more weeks. When she had saved enough money, she bought a train ticket to Cincinnati.

Shooting Match

Cincinnati was the biggest city Annie had ever seen. Lydia and her husband, Joe, showed Annie many interesting places. They even took her to a shooting gallery. Annie hit the targets each time she shot.

"You're wonderful, Annie," Joe said. "There aren't many men who can shoot as well as you can."

"There's one man who can shoot better," Lydia said. "At least he should shoot better. His name is Frank Butler. He does trick shooting at the Coliseum Theater."

"I bet Annie can outshoot him," Joe answered. "Annie, will you have a shooting match with Frank Butler?"

"Sure," Annie said with a grin. "I'll try anything with a gun."

The match was held on Thanksgiving Day in 1876. The prize was 50 dollars. Annie surely wanted to

Cincinnati was a rapidly growing city on the Ohio River when Annie Oakley arrived there in 1876.

win. She did not eat much turkey that day. She wanted to be wide awake when she started shooting.

Annie met Frank Butler at the shooting grounds. They shook hands. Annie thought Frank was the handsomest man she had ever seen. He had a green feather in his cap.

"He looks like Yankee Doodle," Annie thought.

Frank Butler liked Annie too. "What a beautiful little lady!" he said. Annie was fifteen, but she was very short and always would be.

The targets used in the shooting match were called clay pigeons. The pigeons were really just round pieces of clay that looked like saucers. When a shooter cried, "Pull," a clay pigeon was sent flying up in the air. The shooter had to hit it before it touched the ground.

Frank Butler shot first.

"Pull," he cried. The pigeon sailed into the air.

"Bang!" went Frank's gun. The clay pigeon was shattered.

"Dead!" cried the referee. He meant that Frank had hit the target.

Now it was Annie's turn. "It should be easier than hitting quail," she told herself. "When it feels right, I'll shoot."

"Pull!" she ordered. The clay saucer flew high into the air.

"Bang!" Annie's gun went off. She slowly lowered it. "Dead!" cried the referee. Annie had hit the target too.

Both Frank and Annie had to shoot at 25 clay pigeons. The one that hit the most would win. Frank had a turn and hit his clay pigeon. Then Annie had a turn. She hit her pigeon too. And so it went. It began to look as if the match might end in a tie score.

Finally, on the twenty-fifth shot, Frank Butler missed. If Annie could hit the last pigeon, she would win.

"Pull!" Annie cried.

"Dead!" shouted the referee as Annie hit her pigeon.

The crowd cheered wildly. Annie had beaten the great Frank Butler. But Frank did not seem to mind. He went up to Annie and stuck out his hand.

"Well done, Miss Moses," he said, shaking her hand. "I am proud to be beaten by such a good shot."

"Thank you, Mr. Butler," Annie said. "I hope we can have another match."

"I hope so too," Frank answered.

Just then Joe and Lydia rushed up to Annie.

"Come on," Joe cried. "Let's go get your 50 dollars!"

On Stage

Frank Butler often said that he lost both the shooting match and his heart to Annie. And Annie said that she won the match and a husband. For within a year Frank and Annie were married.

Frank had to be at the theater every night for his shooting act. He and his partner, Billy Graham, did many kinds of trick shooting. They had a white-nosed poodle dog named George. At the end of the act, Billy placed an apple on George's head. Then Frank aimed and shot the apple off the dog's head. This always brought loud clapping from the people watching.

Annie often clapped the loudest. She watched the show every night. After it was over, she went back-stage to meet Frank.

One night Billy Graham became very sick just before the act was to begin. The theater was already full of people. Annie was there. Frank sent word for her to come backstage.

"Billy can't be my partner tonight," he said. "You'll have to take his place."

"But I have never been on a stage," Annie said.

"That's nothing. You've been watching every night. You know our act by heart. And you are a better shot than Billy."

When Annie walked out on the stage, the crowd roared with delight. She did all the trick shooting that Billy had done. When it was time to shoot the apple off George's head, Frank made Annie try it.

Annie raised her gun and aimed at the apple. She pulled the trigger. The apple burst into many small pieces. They were scattered about the stage. George started eating the bits of apple. The crowd laughed.

When the curtain fell, Frank said, "They loved you, Annie! From now on you're my partner on stage as well as at home. Together we can make lots of money. People like to see a girl shoot. Few girls shoot well."

"I like shooting on the stage," Annie said. "It's fun!"

"You must have a stage name," Frank said.

"What's wrong with Annie Butler?"

"Your name should be different from mine. Maybe Annie Moses will do."

"Oh, no," Annie cried. "My family wouldn't like me to use their name on the stage."

Frank and Annie talked about many last names. Finally they picked "Oakley."

And so Annie Moses Butler became Annie Oakley on the stage. As "Butler & Oakley," Annie and her husband became a popular shooting team. Wherever they went, Annie was cheered by the crowds.

One day Frank and Annie gave their act before a group of cowboys in Texas.

For some reason Frank could not hit anything. He kept missing a trick shot that was supposed to be his best.

Annie felt sorry for Frank. But there was nothing she could do to help.

Suddenly a big cowboy yelled, "Hey, Butler, get out of here and let the little girl shoot." The cowboy had a gun. It looked as if he might use it on Frank.

"Frank," Annie whispered, "let me try the trick shot." Annie hit the target on her first try. The crowd cheered.

Later Frank said, "Annie, you're a better shot than I can ever be. It's you the people come to see."

"Now Frank," Annie said, "you were a famous shot long before we were married."

"But you are more famous than I am now," said Frank. "I'll be your manager. I'll take care of the business matters. You do the shooting. I'll throw your targets in the air."

"All right," Annie said. "But you are just as important on this team as I am. Don't forget that."

From that time on Annie did all the shooting. After one show the people voted Annie a queen. They named her "The Queen of the Rifle."

Buffalo Bill's Show

One of the most famous buffalo hunters and Indian fighters in America was a man named William S. Cody. He was called "Buffalo Bill." When he stopped fighting Indians, he started a Wild West Show. He wanted people in the eastern part of America to see what the West was really like.

The people who came to his show saw wild buffalo, deer, elk, and bears. They saw Indians wearing warbonnets, with the feathers trailing to the ground.

The show had cowboys who rode bucking horses. There were make-believe bandits who robbed a stage coach. The show also had some men who were good shooters.

Buffalo Bill met Annie and Frank in Kentucky. Annie was so small that Buffalo Bill did not believe she could shoot. When she showed him how good she was with a gun, he changed his mind.

"I wish you'd been with me when I fought the Indians," Buffalo Bill said.

"Would you like me to be in your show?" Annie asked.

"You bet I would," Buffalo Bill said. "All the boys and girls in America will want to see you shoot."

So Annie, with Frank as her manager, joined

BUFFALO BILL'S WILD WEST·
CONGRESS, ROUGH RIDERS OF THE WORLD.

MISS ANNIE OAKLEY,
THE PEERLESS LADY WING-SHOT.

Colorful posters advertised the Wild West Show
and its star performer: "Miss Annie Oakley, the
peerless lady wing-shot."

Buffalo Bill's Wild West Show. From the very start, Buffalo Bill called her "Missie." So Annie got still another name.

Everybody liked Annie's act. She rode into the arena on a snow-white horse. Annie wore a buckskin skirt and shirt. Her chestnut hair flashed below her big cowboy hat. Her blue eyes shone with pleasure.

Frank threw some glass balls into the air. Annie, still on horseback, raised her gun.

"Crack!" With each shot Annie broke a glass ball.

Then Annie got off her horse. Frank held a coin between his thumb and forefinger. Annie shot the coin out of his fingers. Next Frank held up a playing card. Annie shot the spots out of it. Then a wheel with lighted candles started to spin. Annie shot the flames and put the candles out.

The Wild West Show went to many cities. Annie was popular in all of them.

Years before, Buffalo Bill had fought against Sitting Bull, the great Sioux Indian chief. Now he and Sitting Bull were friends. Buffalo Bill asked Sitting Bull to join the Wild West Show.

Sitting Bull looked more like an eagle than a bull. He had a big beak-like nose and dark eyes. His chest was almost as big as a barrel.

When Sitting Bull saw Annie shoot, he grunted

with pleasure. Annie reminded him of his own daughter who had died many years before. Sitting Bull came to Annie's tent.

"You are like my own daughter," he said. "Will you be my adopted daughter? I will make you a member of the Sioux tribe."

"Thank you," Annie said. "I've already had one real father and two stepfathers. I guess I can have one more father."

Sitting Bull lit his peace pipe. He blew a puff of smoke over Annie's head.

"I name you Wan-tan-yeya Ci-sci-la," Sitting Bull said. In the Sioux language, that means "Little Sureshot."

That was the way Annie got still another name. Years later, when Sitting Bull died, he left all his possessions to Little Sureshot, his adopted daughter. Among them were his moccasins, his peace pipe, and his council stick.

Kings and Queens

One night after a show in New York, Annie told Frank some exciting news.

"Buffalo Bill had a letter from Mark Twain today! Think of it—from Mark Twain!" Mark Twain was the famous author of *Tom Sawyer*.

"What did he say in the letter?" Frank asked her. "Mr. Twain said the Wild West Show should go to England. He said our show is real to the last detail. It will show people in England what the West is like."

One spring day in 1887, the Wild West Show sailed for England. The ship was named the *State of Nebraska*.

On board were more than 200 cowboys, Indians, and Mexicans. There were also many horses, buffalo, elk, deer, bears, and antelope. Someone said the ship should be called *The Ark*.

It was a rough trip. Many cowboys and Indians were seasick, but Annie felt fine all the way. When the ship sailed up the river to London, Annie and Frank were standing on deck. A tugboat, flying the American flag, came to welcome the Wild West Show to England.

The Prince and Princess of Wales came to see the show in London. Someday they would be the king and queen of England. The prince was thrilled by Annie's trick shooting. He and the princess came to see Annie after the show.

"I wish we had a thousand girls just like you in the English army," the prince said. "You are the best shot in the world."

Later, Queen Victoria, the prince's mother, came

to the show. She brought some kings and queens who were visiting her from other countries.

Buffalo Bill, riding on his horse, led the grand parade. He was waving a large American flag. Behind him, on their horses, came the cowboys and the Indians.

The Indian braves were colorful in their feathered headdresses and war paint. The cowboys and the Indians broke the silence with yells and war whoops.

The whole company lined up with Buffalo Bill before the queen. The cowboys held their hats high in the air.

The queen stood up. Then she bowed her head to the American flag.

"Yi-peeee!" the cowboys screamed. Their yells could be heard for miles. It was a wonderful thing for the queen to do. Then the queen sat down. Buffalo Bill and the cowboys and the Indians left.

Suddenly Annie Oakley galloped in. The spotlights followed her to the center of the ring. Her helper threw three glass balls into the air.

"Bang! Bang! Bang!" Annie hit them all.

Next Annie jumped from her horse. Five more glass balls were thrown high above her head. Annie quickly turned a handspring. She jumped over a table. Then she grabbed a gun and broke the glass

Firing at targets as she stood on the back of a
galloping horse became Annie's special act.

balls before they hit the ground. The cheers were
deafening. Annie bowed to the crowd and left.

Then a herd of buffalo, chased by cowboys, ran
into the ring.

After the show, Annie met Queen Victoria. Her
son, Prince Edward, was standing beside her. The
queen asked Annie how old she was when she
learned to shoot. Annie told her. The queen said,
"You are a very clever little girl."

"Thank you, Your Majesty," Annie said politely.

A young lord spoke to Annie. "Don't you feel
nervous shooting before kings and queens?"

"Why, no," Annie answered, giving him a friendly smile. "I have shot before thousands of American boys and girls."

The lord blushed, but the prince laughed. He knew it was Annie's way of saying that she thought American boys and girls were just as important as kings and queens.

Annie was very popular in England. Four men asked her to marry them. People did not know she had a husband, for she used the name "Annie Oakley" instead of Mrs. Frank Butler.

One man sent Annie his picture. He said he wanted to marry her. Annie thought it was funny. She used the picture for a target. She shot several holes through the picture of the man's head. Then she sent the picture back to him.

When she told Frank, he roared with laughter. "That will teach him to leave my Annie alone," he said happily.

A Diamond Pin

After the show closed in London, Annie and Frank went to Germany. Annie had been invited to shoot before the German king who was called the kaiser.

A big crowd came to see Annie shoot. Then a message arrived from the kaiser. He was too sick to come. This made the crowd sad. Annie was disappointed too.

At first the crowd watched her shooting in icy silence. Annie hit target after target. Slowly the ice began to melt. Annie hit six targets that were thrown in the air at once.

The crowd clapped loudly. Prince William, the kaiser's grandson, walked up to Annie.

"Miss Oakley," he said, "in London, you shot the ashes off a cigarette held in your helper's mouth."

"That's right," Annie said.

"I would like you to do that trick here," the prince said. "I will be your helper."

What could Annie do? She hated to refuse the prince. What if she missed the cigarette and hit the prince in the head?

Before she could think of an excuse, the prince lit a cigarette. He held it between his lips. Annie swung her gun to her shoulder and took careful aim. Then she pulled the trigger. The ashes on the prince's cigarette fell to the ground. The crowd cheered for a long time.

After leaving Germany, Annie and Frank came back to America. Annie did trick shooting in the Wild West Show for many more years. Then she went back to Europe with the Wild West Show. They traveled in France and other countries.

Annie Oakley and one of the Indian performers in
Buffalo Bill's Wild West Show

Once Annie was in Vienna. A rich baroness asked her to give a show to raise money to help some orphans. Annie remembered the orphans she knew when she lived with the Eddingtons. She was glad to help the baroness raise money for the children.

Annie's show for the orphans in Vienna was a big success. A lot of money was raised. To thank Annie, the baroness sent her a bag full of gold coins. Annie gave the gold coins to the orphans.

The baroness soon heard about Annie's gift to the orphans. She was so pleased that she sent Annie a big diamond pin. The pin sparkled like fire when Annie wore it.

Annie's Last Show

One night in 1901, Annie and Frank were on the Wild West Show train. It was going from Charlotte, North Carolina, to Danville, Virginia.

Annie and Frank were sound asleep. Suddenly they were awakened by a terrible crash.

"Are you all right, Annie?" Frank yelled.

"I think so, Frank," Annie answered.

The show train had hit a freight train. Both trains were wrecked. Nearly all the Wild West Show horses were killed. Nobody died, but many were hurt. And Annie was not "all right." She was badly hurt. She had to wear a brace on her right leg for a long time.

Annie had to leave the Wild West Show. She and Frank bought a house in Nutley, New Jersey.

Everyone who had seen the Wild West Show when Annie was in it missed her. A newspaperman reported, "Where, oh, where is Annie Oakley? It does not seem quite the same old shooting match without Miss Oakley potting pigeons in the ring."

Annie did not know if she would ever be able to shoot again. One day she took her gun and went into the woods. Frank and their dog went with her. Annie was still on crutches. But she wanted to see if she could still shoot.

Frank threw a coin into the air. Annie raised her gun to her shoulder. When it felt right, she pulled the trigger.

"Ping!" the coin rang when Annie hit it. She was still "Little Sureshot."

Annie started giving shooting shows again. She also taught other people how to shoot. She loved to teach children.

When America was at war with Germany, Annie wanted to join the army. She probably would have made a good soldier. But she knew the army would not enlist a woman.

However, Annie did help win the war. She visited

many army training camps. Annie showed young soldiers how easy shooting was.

"If I can shoot," Annie said, "you boys can shoot."

Finally the war was over. Many American soldiers had been killed and hurt. Annie was asked to help raise money for those who returned. People would still pay to see her shoot.

"I'm afraid I can't shoot the way I used to," Annie said. "But I am willing to try."

People who saw her said she had never been better. Frank Butler swung a ball on a cord around his head. Annie held her gun in her left hand. With her back toward Frank, she took aim in a mirror held in her right hand. She pulled the trigger. The bullet cut the cord. The ball sailed away.

Next Annie leaned backward over a chair and tossed three glass balls over her head. She grabbed a gun and broke each ball to bits.

"Hurrah for Annie Oakley," the crowd screamed. The next day a newspaper said, "Miss Annie Oakley was the hit of the afternoon." Annie had hit just about everything with her gun.

Annie Oakley was still the shooting star. But her long, exciting life was near its end. Two years later, in 1926, Annie died quietly at the home of a friend.

Like a shooting star in the sky, Annie Oakley's light went out.

Why Not Women?

Little Annie Oakley outrode and outshot her male com-
petitors—and delighted the audiences who thronged to see
her perform in Buffalo Bill's Wild West Show. Annie just had
to be a sharpshooter because that's what she did best.

In recent years other women, too, have asked for a
chance to enter sports in which they felt they could excel.
What if these were in fields occupied only by men? They
have asked quite matter-of-factly, "Why *not* women?" and
proceeded—often under protest—to prove their point.

Kathy Kusner (right) and Penny Ann Early (below) are pioneers who fought for the right to ride as professional jockeys. Penny worked for several years as an exercise girl at a race track. Kathy was an Olympics equestrienne and a prizewinning rider at horse shows.

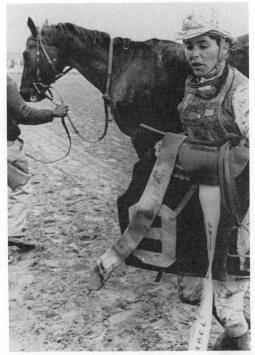

Some of the players on New York's first women's professional football team, the New York Fillies, do calisthenics at a practice session (left) and play their first game (below) against a team from Detroit.

Paula Murphy became "the
fastest woman on wheels"
in 1964 when she blasted
her racer to a top speed
of 226 miles per hour on
Bonneville Salt Flats,
Utah. Paula is seen here
in her jet-powered racer
called the *Avenger*.

MARIA MITCHELL
1818–1889

charted the stars from the rooftop of
her Nantucket home when she was a
girl. As Maria grew older, she became her astronomer-father's trusted
assistant. Finally, she discovered in
the autumn skies of Nantucket a new
comet! In time, Maria's comet brought
her a gold medal and the proud title
of "astronomer." Maria became a
famous scientist in the days when
few women had the opportunity to
learn more than "reading, writing, and
arithmetic." She joined scientific
societies. She visited the famous
astronomers of Europe. And she became the first professor of astronomy
at Matthew Vassar's new college for
women. Here Maria Mitchell taught
her students how to look at the universe. Even more important, she
taught them how to look at themselves as women with an active role
to play in the world outside Vassar's
walls.

Maria Mitchell

Stargazer

by *Katharine E. Wilkie*

Copyright © 1966 by Katharine E. Wilkie

The Eclipse

February 19, 1831, was a cold day in Nantucket. Maria Mitchell slipped away from her brothers and sisters playing in the yard. She went into the gray-shingled house at Number 1 Vestal Street.

She stopped in the doorway. Her eyes grew large. Father had taken out a window and set his telescope in the opening. He looked up and saw her.

"The better to see the eclipse of the sun," he told her.

The girl sat down at a small table. It held a chronometer, or ship's clock. Maria would help her father in making his observations of the eclipse.

Most of the people on Nantucket Island knew something about astronomy. The Massachusetts island was a great whaling center. The sailors used the stars to steer by.

William Mitchell was not a sailor. He worked at many jobs—farmer, teacher, and banker. But his great love was astronomy. There was no better astronomer on the island.

Now he looked away from the telescope. He saw

the youngsters running about outside. He winked at Maria.

"Just look at all those children!" he said to mother. "Thee had better send home those that do not belong to us and call the rest in."

Mother's mouth flew open. She did not always know when father was teasing.

"They are *all* ours, William."

Father's eyes twinkled. "Thee does not say!"

Maria felt warm and happy inside. Although father was a Quaker and used Quaker speech, he loved to laugh and joke. He loved gay colors too. There were red roses on the wallpaper. There was a glass globe hanging from the ceiling. He used it in his science experiments. It separated rays of light into every color of the rainbow.

Just then the other young Mitchells came trooping in. Father shook his head at them, and they became quiet as mice.

Maria counted the seconds on the chronometer as the children watched.

"One–two–three–four . . ."

The bright winter sunlight was growing paler. It was not yet noon, but it seemed much later. A strange stillness came over the island of Nantucket. The light became dimmer.

"Just look!" said Sally, the eldest daughter. "The

chickens are going to roost. They think night is coming on."

Maria was still counting. "Twenty-three . . . twenty-four . . . twenty-five . . ."

"Thee must look through the piece of smoked glass so the sun will not hurt thy eyes," Ann warned little Phebe.

A curved disk had begun to appear on the edge of the glowing sun. It looked like the edge of a big penny.

"Mark!" father exclaimed.

"Eleven fifty-five," Maria announced.

The eclipse had begun. The shadow of the moon on the sun grew larger and larger. Soon the shadow would cover the sun. The family could hardly see the white picket fence outside.

Each young Mitchell had a turn at the telescope. "Look carefully," father said. "There will not be another eclipse visible in Nantucket for many years."

Slowly the black circle began to slip away. Now the darkness turned to half darkness. In the distance a rooster was crowing. In a short time the full sun was shining brightly.

The children went back to their play outside. Only Maria remained indoors.

"Let us take the telescope back to the attic," she suggested. "If the wind dies down, we may be able to watch the stars from the walk on the rooftop tonight."

The *walk* was a railed platform on the roof of a house. People in Nantucket usually went up to the walk to watch ships coming and going in the harbor.

William Mitchell loved the hours up on the walk as much as Maria did. He always looked forward to viewing the heavens with his young helper.

On the Housetop

Maria dried the supper dishes quickly. Then she scampered up the steep stairs to the attic. A cold night wind blew against her face as she stepped out on the walk.

Father had placed the telescope close to the great chimney. Maria sat down beside him. She looked out over the housetops. In the distance, ships of all shapes and sizes were riding at anchor in the moonlight.

"I should like to sail on a whaling ship," Maria said. "A ship in the middle of the ocean would be a grand place to view the heavens on a clear night."

Father laughed. "No better than the roof at Number 1 Vestal Street. And what would I do without my prize pupil? Maria, thee is becoming a fine

This early drawing shows Nantucket as it looked when Maria Mitchell was a girl.

astronomer. Could thee teach the younger children what I have taught thee?"

"I am doing it," Maria said. "Last night when thee was at meeting, I brought Ann up here. We used the telescope. We were very careful. Was that wrong?"

Father shook his head. Maria went on talking.

"Ann never gets tired of those old stories about the Greeks and Romans. She likes to hear about the gods and goddesses that the heavenly bodies are named for. She begs me to tell the stories over and over again."

By now Maria's dark eyes were shining. She loved to share with others what her father had taught her.

"There is so much to know," Maria went on, "and I know so little. Those stars out yonder seem so unchanging. It is as if they are part of a Great Plan."

"The astronomer who does not believe in God must be mad," father said. He rose to his feet. "Would thee care to view the moons of Jupiter?"

Maria moved over eagerly. She watched the four small moons of the planet Jupiter. Then she turned the telescope on Saturn.

For Maria the hours on the rooftop flew by like minutes. Maria loved ordinary good times too. She liked to wander on the beach and collect shells and pebbles. She liked to make up stories and poems for her brothers and sisters. And she enjoyed her studies at school, especially arithmetic.

One had to be good at arithmetic to measure the positions of the stars. And it was the stars that she loved most of all. They were so regular and unchanging.

Lost on the Moor

Maria and her brother Andrew were standing on the wharves. They had just come from a visit to their Uncle Isaac's whaling ship, the *Ann*. It was a graceful, high-masted sailing vessel. Uncle Isaac had shown them over the ship from the foredeck to the galleys.

"I could use a strong, willing lad like you," he told Andrew. "A sailor should start young and grow up on shipboard."

"I am strong and willing," Maria teased. "Why don't you take me?" How she wished she could be a boy and go adventuring!

Uncle Isaac laughed. "A captain's wife can go to sea. You had better plan to become a captain's wife."

Maria's black eyes snapped. "Maybe I don't want to be anybody's wife. Maybe I'd rather be one of the crew."

Now Maria and Andrew were back on land. Andrew looked wistfully at the ship they had just left.

"She is a beauty," he said. "If only I were sailing on her tomorrow morning!"

"Father would never consent," Maria reminded him. And she was glad. Next to father, Andrew was her favorite companion.

The next morning when the family awakened, Andrew's bed was empty. A note was pinned to his pillow. It read: "I have gone off to sea on the *Ann* with Uncle Isaac. Thy loving son, Andrew."

A dreadful scene followed. Mother cried. Father

remained tight-lipped and silent. Soon after break-fast he went out to the fields with his plow.

After Maria had finished her morning chores, she walked on the beach and thought of Andrew. Some-times whaling vessels were gone two years. Finally she left the shore and turned inland. She and Andrew had often wandered on the wild, lonely moor together. After a while she felt better.

Maria sat down to eat her lunch. A tiny green snake slithered across her foot. A saucy chipmunk stopped beside her. She was a long way from where she had started.

Suddenly a drop of water hit her nose. She looked up in surprise. The skies were dark. Big thunder-clouds had piled up. The island was in for a blow.

It grew darker each minute. She was too far from home to turn back. Far in the distance she saw a faint light.

"It must mean shelter," she thought. She made her way through the blinding rain. At last she came to a tumbledown hut. She rapped at the door. There was no answer. Then she pushed open the door and stumbled in.

For a moment she wished she had stayed outside. Three old women by the smoking fire stared at her.

There was a sharp flash of lightning. A peal of

thunder followed. Maria recalled father's deep voice as he read aloud the witches' scene from *Macbeth:*

When shall we three meet again
In thunder, lightning, or in rain?

She wished she were back on Vestal Street where roses covered the wallpaper in the sitting room.

One of the old women got up. "I know thee, Maria Mitchell. Why is thee so far from home?"

Maria felt better. The old woman had used Quaker speech. Now she remembered the three. They were the Newbigin sisters: Anna, Mary, and Phebe. Each First Day, or Sunday, they came to meeting. They sat like ragged scarecrows through the service.

"Take a chair and dry thy clothes, child," Anna told her.

Mary was stirring something in an iron kettle over the fire. She handed Maria a bowl of thin soup. All three watched the girl drink every mouthful.

There were cobwebs hanging from the ceiling. There was dirt in every corner. Maria wished she had never come.

Soon the storm grew milder. She rose to go.

"Thee should spend the night," Phebe told her. "'Tis a bad time to lose one's way."

"No, thank thee," Maria replied politely. "I must go." She stumbled outdoors and drew in great breaths of fresh air. She did not stop running until she had left the hut far behind.

But where was home? There was no moon out tonight. Clouds hid the stars. She felt bewildered. Then the clouds parted. In a short time the moon shone through. The sky was as clear as if it had never rained.

Maria studied the friendly stars. "There is the North Star!" she exclaimed. "The town of Nantucket lies on the north side of the island. The North Star will take me to the coast. Then I can find my way home. I know the coastline almost as well as the stars."

Maria Teaches School

Maria was seventeen now. She was the oldest daughter at home. Sally had married. Andrew had come home from sea and become a farmer.

But there were still six young Mitchells at home. Father did not have a large income. A family of eight needed money to live, and Maria was eager to help.

"I shall open a school," Maria said to her father one day.

Mr. Mitchell nodded. "Thee is a born teacher. I have watched thee with thy younger brothers and sisters."

"I want to teach children to think. I want to awaken them to ask questions and to wonder about everything, just as thee has taught me," Maria said.

On September 1, 1835, Maria waited in a vacant house on Trader's Lane. Her heart was pounding. Would any children come to her school?

A shadow fell across the doorway. A small dark-skinned girl stood there. Maria knew at once where she was from. She came from a settlement called "Little Egypt," down by the wharves. Both Portuguese and black people lived there.

Many Nantucketers disapproved of these dark-skinned people. They lived in shabby fishermen's huts. People forgot that fishermen's wages were small.

Maria Mitchell smiled at the little Portuguese girl.

"May I come in?" the child asked. Her voice was very low. "My name is Lisa," she said.

"Of course you may come in," Maria told Lisa. "You are my first pupil, and I am glad to see you."

Before the day was over, some more children had come. There were black children, Portuguese, and

Quakers. The Quaker children wore grays and blacks. They looked like dull moths beside the brightly dressed children from Little Egypt.

From the first, Maria's school was different. There were not enough books for everyone, but there was the whole outdoors to study.

"Learn to see the world about you," Maria told them. "Nature is the great teacher. Learn from her."

Her school did not always have regular hours. Early risers sometimes saw Maria and her flock setting out at daybreak. They were on their way to watch baby birds being hatched.

Many nights she crowded her pupils onto the walk on the rooftop of her home. There, through the telescope, they saw the glory of the heavens.

Often, in the daytime, they went to the beach. On the sand Maria drew maps of far-off places. Names like Cape Horn, Malaya, the Azores, and New Guinea were everyday words to the little Nantucketers. They had heard them many times from their fathers and brothers, when they came home after a long voyage.

But gradually the children stopped coming to the school. Finally Maria's school closed its doors.

Soon after that, in 1836, Maria was offered the job of librarian at the Atheneum, the town's handsome new library.

"It can't be true!" she told her father. "They will pay me money just to work with books. I would rather be with books than anywhere else in the world—except on the rooftop with thee and the telescope."

Maria's cheeks were rosy with excitement. Some folks thought her plain, but she was almost beautiful now.

"The Atheneum will not be open to the public in the morning," Maria said. "I can study there then. There will be books on poetry, philosophy, physics, navigation, and astronomy itself. I can hardly wait."

"I wish thee could go to college," her father said sadly. "Thee has the mind for it. But almost no colleges accept women. I am too poor to pay thy way if they did."

"Thee must not mind," Maria told him. "The Atheneum shall be my college. The great minds of the centuries shall be my daily companions. Isn't that what college really means?"

The Big Fire

Something else happened in 1836. Father became cashier of the Pacific Bank. The Mitchells moved into the apartment above the bank. Their hard times were over.

Father built a wooden shelter for the telescope on the rooftop. By now he had become a well-known astronomer. He was a friend of William Bond, head of the Harvard Observatory. West Point had lent father special instruments. He built two little houses behind the bank for them.

And that was not all. The director of the Coast Survey sent him more equipment, including a special telescope. For some time now father had been making astronomical observations for the government.

The new telescope meant as much to Maria as to her father. Maria had become a skilled astronomer herself. She helped her father with his observations.

"Maria's eyes are amazingly sensitive to color and to form," her father said. "She notices the slightest change in a star."

One night when Maria was in bed, she was awakened by loud shouts of "Fire! Fire!" She rushed to the window and looked out. For a moment she thought the whole town was ablaze.

"What happened?" she called down to a man on the street.

"The hat shop caught on fire," he shouted back. "The flames spread to some oil casks. Now the fire seems to be everywhere."

Maria joined her mother and sisters at the front entrance of the bank. Every able-bodied man and boy had joined the bucket brigade. They were working with all their might to save as much as they could.

The flames swept nearer. They almost reached the wooden church down the street.

Mother groaned. "If the church goes, the bank will be next, and who knows where the fire will stop."

Men from government ships were standing by. Their leader was about to order them to blow up the church. He thought that would keep the fire from spreading.

Maria could not bear to see the beautiful building with the tall white columns destroyed. Like an angel of wrath, she flew up the steps of the church. She spread her arms between two of the columns.

"I dare you to touch it!" she cried.

The men fell back. Maria was in earnest. Just then the wind changed. The flames went another way. The church and the bank were safe.

But the sparks had set fire to the little observatory on the roof of the bank building. Maria and her brother Henry, together with their father, rushed up there and beat out the flames.

But the instruments were damaged, and the records were lost. Months and years of work had gone up in flames in a few minutes.

While the Mitchell family was trying to save the

The people of Nantucket fight the Main Street fire with buckets and hand pumpers.

observatory, the Atheneum caught fire. All the books in the library were destroyed.

The people of Nantucket wasted no time in feeling sorry for themselves. New buildings rose on Main Street to replace the old ones. There was soon a new Atheneum. And Maria was in charge of buying the books.

"Let us secure not such books as people want, but books just above their wants, and they will reach up to take what is put out for them," she said.

But her heart was with astronomy. Luckily not all the equipment had been damaged by the fire. And father built a new observatory. Every clear night Maria was in her old place on the rooftop.

111

Maria Discovers a Comet

It had been a long day at the Atheneum. Maria found a half dozen guests in the parlor when she returned to her home.

She soon left them and slipped away to the observatory. It was a perfect autumn night for sweeping the skies. She looked at the logbook and noted the measurements she and her father had made the night before.

She turned the telescope and looked at Orion. Then through the lens she sighted the star group called the Corona Borealis.

Downstairs she could hear laughter and talking. She was tired. She was glad to be up here alone with the stars.

Suddenly she stiffened. There in the upper part of the field of the telescope was a tiny white spot. She knew that part of the heavens as well as she knew the Atheneum. No white spot should be there.

She turned her head and closed her eyes. Could they be tricking her? Then she looked again through the lens. The white spot was still there. The chronometer showed that the time was exactly half past ten. She wrote down the figures.

Then she rose and hurried down the narrow attic stairs to find her father. She must be sure!

The guests stopped talking as she rushed into the room. Mr. Mitchell looked up.

"Come quickly, father!" she begged.

She turned and flew back up the stairs. Father was close behind. Mother, sister Kate, and the guests followed.

Up on the rooftop William Mitchell looked carefully through the lens. He shook his head and turned away. Then he looked again for a long time.

With a proud smile he turned to the others and spoke.

"My friends, I believe my daughter has discovered a new comet on this night of October 1, 1847."

That night Mr. Mitchell wrote to his old friend Professor Bond at Harvard University. Before long a letter from the professor arrived. He had used Maria's reckoning and found the comet with his telescope.

Father waved the letter. "I *told* thee! Soon the whole world will be hearing of thy comet."

"Do not call it *my* comet," Maria answered.

"Why not? A comet is always named for the person who discovers it. Thee will soon be hearing more. Professor Bond has sent a notice to a German journal which announces all such discoveries."

Day after day passed. At last father had another letter.

"Just listen to this!" he exclaimed. "Professor Bond writes: 'It seems that Maria Mitchell's comet has not been seen before in Europe.'" He looked proudly at his daughter. "Twenty-nine years old and already thee has become a famous astronomer!"

"Thee has taught me all I know," Maria told him. "It is as much thy discovery as mine."

Mother sniffed. "Whenever you stop admiring each other, there is work to be done." But she looked proud too.

In 1831 the king of Denmark had promised a gold medal to the first discoverer of a "telescopic comet." This kind of comet is visible only through a telescope.

Was Maria the first to announce the discovery of the comet? There seemed some doubt. Her father's letter had been delayed by a storm. The ship carrying the mail left Nantucket three days after Maria's discovery. A man in Rome had seen the comet on October 3. Who had announced it first?

Even the president of Harvard was drawn into the question. So was the astronomer royal of Great Britain. So were other important people in America and Denmark.

At last on October 6, 1848, the king of Denmark awarded the medal to Maria. It was a great day for her when it arrived in a little velvet box.

There were tears in her eyes as she looked at it. On one side of the medal was the likeness of the king of Denmark. On the other side in Latin were the words: "Not in vain do we watch the setting and rising of the stars."

Under the words was the date: October 1, 1847. MARIA MITCHELL was printed in large letters around the edge.

"Now thee is beginning thy career," William Mitchell told her.

She shook her head. "I began it long ago when thee first taught me the wonder of the stars."

Maria Goes to Europe

"I can't believe I am really going to Europe," Maria said.

"No one deserves it more than thee," father told her. "Thee has been the backbone of this family long enough."

It was 1857. Maria was no longer a girl. Nine years had passed since she had received the medal from the king of Denmark. That honor had brought her fame. Soon she was made a member of several important scientific societies.

To her surprise she was asked to help with the work of the new *American Ephemeris and Nautical*

Almanac. An ephemeris is the name for tables showing the positions of heavenly bodies at regular periods of time. For many years England had had one. America had used it. Now she would have one of her own. Maria would compute the tables of Venus for it.

That same year she was invited with her young brother Henry to do special astronomical work at a camp in Maine. The camp was held by the director of the Coast Survey. Neither Maria nor her brother ever forgot those peaceful nights under the stars.

Now the time had come for Maria to leave for Europe. Her married sisters had come to say goodbye.

"Look after mother," Maria said to her sisters.

Mother was feeble now, but she had not lost her spirit.

"I shall take care of myself," she announced.

Maria left Nantucket in a shower of good wishes. Wonderful days lay ahead.

In England she saw all the sights—cathedrals, museums, castles, and palaces. She visited the homes of poets and playwrights whose works she had read and loved. She even tracked down an old house where Isaac Newton had once lived. He was the famous scientist who had discovered the laws of gravitation.

It was hard for Maria to realize that she herself was famous. All the leading British scientists wanted to meet her. She visited the astronomer Sir John Herschel in his home. Every evening they talked about astronomy until dawn.

From England Maria went to France and then on to Italy. She was enchanted by Rome. Her greatest wish was to visit the Vatican Observatory. No woman had ever been there. Maria asked permission and received it.

"You never get anything if you don't ask for it," she said with simple New England frankness.

It was a thrilling moment when she stood on the spot where Galileo had been tried centuries before by the Church. He had been forced to deny his belief that the planets revolve around the sun. In his day most people believed that the earth was the center of the universe. They felt it was against the Christian faith to think otherwise.

"How strange that some people cannot believe in both the Book of Nature and the Book of God," Maria said softly to herself.

Before she left Italy, Maria visited Mary Somerville. Years before, that lady had translated into English a great French book on astronomy.

Mrs. Somerville was old now, but her mind had stayed young. She talked with her visitor about everything from the stars to chemistry, and even about the recent discovery of gold in California.

Maria smiled to herself. "And to think some people believe women should only cook and sew. Thank goodness father felt I had a mind and taught me to use it."

Maria was glad to be going home. She missed her father and their nights viewing the stars from the walk on the rooftop. She missed all her family. She was hungry for a bowl of New England chowder. And she wanted to feel the winds of Nantucket on her face.

Vassar Calls

Soon after Maria returned to America, her mother died. Maria and her father moved to Lynn, Massachusetts, near Boston. Maria's sister Kate lived there with her husband and their children.

The years at Lynn were happy years. Family and friends always seemed to gather at the Mitchell cottage. Maria had a handsome new telescope given her by the "Women of America." It was housed in a shelter in the backyard. Her father still worked with her.

One day in 1862 they had a visitor. He was sent by a rich man named Matthew Vassar. Mr. Vassar was just starting a college for women in New York State. It would open as soon as it could be built.

Mr. Vassar's messenger sat for a long time in the garden with Maria and her father. He told the father and daughter about the college.

"Vassar will have fine equipment, an excellent library, and the best teachers. It will have an observatory," he said.

He stole a glance at Maria. She looked interested.

"Matthew Vassar wants you to be professor of astronomy," he told her.

"That is impossible!" Maria exclaimed. "I don't even have a college degree."

"Yes, she does," her father said. "Hanover College gave her an honorary degree in 1853."

Their visitor smiled. "It does not matter about a college degree. Mr. Vassar feels that you are the best person in the world to hold the position."

Maria felt very happy. Mr. Vassar believed in women. He believed in her. She would have a part in the new college right from the start.

But her happiness did not last long. Many people opposed Mr. Vassar's ideas.

"Women are too delicate to attend college," one educator thundered.

"Women cannot perform worthwhile mental tasks," another said.

Maria was angry when she heard such talk. She read everything the newspapers had to say about education for women. Some men were sure that a woman's place was in the home. Others thought she should take her place in the outside world. Some did not know what they thought, but they spoke anyway.

Meanwhile Maria waited eagerly for the new college to open its doors. But it did not open as soon as she had hoped. The Civil War delayed the opening. There was little time to build a school while a war was going on.

September 20, 1865, was the opening day of Vassar College. Maria and her father had already moved into their living quarters in the observatory at Vassar.

Now the young ladies arrived. Maria could hardly wait to teach in the fine new observatory with its twelve-inch telescope.

At last she stood before her first class. All of the girls had heard of Maria Mitchell. She was famous. They watched the tall woman with gray curls who looked at them intently before she began to speak.

"I do not expect to make great mathematicians or astronomers of you. But I want you to open your eyes to the universe about you," she said.

When she saw their wide-awake faces, she laid

down her notes and just talked to them. She took them back with her to the long-ago days of her childhood in Nantucket. She told them about the housetop of a gray-shingled house on Vestal Street. There she let them share a little girl's wonder at the vast night sky.

"We know so little, but we must keep on asking," she finished. "What makes a *nova*? Why are there double stars? Is there life on other planets? Does space ever end?"

A tall, dark-eyed girl stayed behind after the others had left. Her eyes were shining. Maria learned that

Maria Mitchell (second from left) and her pupils study astronomy on the lawn at Vassar College.

the girl's name was Mary Whitney. She could not know that one day the girl would follow her as professor of astronomy at Vassar.

Maria Mitchell was herself at all times. She was honest. She was friendly. Her classes were exciting.

At Vassar everyone changed for dinner. Maria thought this was a great waste of time. One evening a new student stepped on the hem of Maria's dress and promptly burst into tears.

"Don't cry or apologize," Maria said quickly. "I should never have worn the thing in the first place."

A shower of meteors, "shooting stars," was predicted for November 15, 1866.

When it began, Maria did not heed the school rule that "no gas should be lit after ten o'clock."

Instead, she ran up and down the hall, lighting gas jets and calling to the girls. The principal was furious, but Maria did not care. Her girls must not miss this tremendous event.

Another time she waited for a comet which could be seen through the telescope only late at night. She looked through the finder. She saw that a half-dead apple tree was in the way.

There was no time to lose. She called the school handyman and pointed to the tree.

"Cut it down!" she ordered.

When Maria went down to breakfast the next morning, her delighted pupils chorused: "Good morning, George Washington!"

Life was never dull, not even for a minute, around Maria Mitchell.

The Later Years

William Mitchell died in 1869. Maria was heartbroken. Her many friends tried to help her fill the lonely hours. Louisa May Alcott visited her at Vassar, and so did Julia Ward Howe.

Maria worked harder than ever at her teaching. She wrote magazine articles, too, and became a popular speaker all over the East. She worked to advance the cause of education for women.

Maria was growing old in years, but her mind was as young as ever. She was the first astronomer in America to make a series of photographs of the sun's surface. She also made special studies of the planets Jupiter and Saturn.

In June 1888 Maria held a "dome party" in the observatory at Vassar. She had been famous for her dome parties for 20 years.

Maria looked about at the happy laughing girls.

"You don't look as though college has injured your health," she told them.

This photograph of Maria Mitchell (seated) and
Mary Whitney was taken in the Vassar observatory.

"College injure our health? How could it?" a girl asked.

"When Vassar was started, many people were upset," she told them. "They foretold an early end for girls in a man's world."

The girls laughed harder than ever.

"They really believed it," Maria insisted. "But they were wrong. Today there are many colleges for girls."

"But none more interesting than Vassar," Maria continued. "For years I have watched Vassar girls grow into the best-educated persons in the world. Someday women like you will be allowed to vote. Go out into the world now and hurry that day along."

A hush fell upon the girls. Maria Mitchell always brought out the highest and best in them.

Maria Mitchell stayed on at Vassar until the following Christmas. Then she retired and went home to Lynn. There, behind her cottage, her architect-nephew had built her a small observatory. Maria worked there until her death on June 28, 1889.

Today visitors come from all over the world to the Maria Mitchell Museum at Number 1 Vestal Street in Nantucket. It was once the gray-shingled home of a Quaker child who wondered about everything in the world and grew up to be the first woman astronomer in America.

The Wide World
Is Their Laboratory

Botanist-oceanographer SYLVIA A. EARLE lived underwater for two weeks in July 1970 as the leader of a team of five adventurous women aquanauts. The aquanauts—four scientists and one electrical engineer—were trained over a period of time to live and work on the floor of the Caribbean Sea. Their object: to collect information on plant and animal life for the U. S. government's Tektite project. Dr. Earle and the other members of her team rested, ate, slept, and prepared their specimens in the Habitat, a four-chambered "apartment" resting fifty feet below the surface of the sea. Intensive preparation for the project included hours of briefing, training in scuba diving, and in the operation of the Habitat control systems. They also learned thoroughly the "geography" of the ocean floor to enable them to get back to their underwater home. Their watchword when in trouble was "Never panic—think!"

When physiologist MARGARET JACKSON first became interested in space flight in 1941, she put on a space suit and helmet and climbed into an Air Force C131-B aircraft to find out for herself the effects of weightlessness on human beings. As the plane swooped down fast enough to change the pull of gravity to zero, she became the first woman ever to experience weightlessness. Her work since then has taken her to NASA's Manned Spacecraft Center in Houston, Texas, where she has worked on the problems of breathing in space. In a series of experiments Miss Jackson and other scientists have tested the reactions of human beings to spacelike conditions. The results of these tests help them decide how to provide the best kind of atmosphere for astronauts working and resting in space. Margaret Jackson is one of the many women scientists who, though earthbound, have helped to send others into space.

Ethologist JANE VAN LAWICK-GOODALL left school in England at eighteen and went to work as a secretary, planning to earn enough money to pay her fare to Africa. There she hoped to study animals in the grasslands and jungles where they lived. Adventurous Jane's fondest dream came true when she did indeed manage to make the trip to Africa. At the suggestion of a famous scientist, Jane set off for the Gombe Stream Reserve to study the behavior of the 100 or more chimpanzees who lived there. At first the chimpanzees at the reserve ran away when she came near them, but as time went on, they became more and more friendly. Soon she was able to move freely among them, recording every detail of their daily life. Jane's research on the Gombe Reserve provided important information for other scientists. It was recorded in a National Geographic Society film entitled *Miss Goodall and the Chimpanzees* and in her own book, *My Friends the Wild Chimpanzees.* She is married to Baron Hugo van Lawick whose photographs illustrate her book.

Biologist-author RACHEL CARSON loved the sea and the earth and hoped to preserve their goodness for all mankind. As a young girl growing up in rural Pennsylvania, she experienced all the delights of the outdoors. Rachel majored in science in college and, after graduating, spent the summer working in constant sight and sound of the sea at the Marine Biological Laboratory in Woods Hole, Massachusetts. After several years of graduate work, she was hired by the U. S. Bureau of Fisheries—the first woman scientist ever to work for this agency. As part of her job, she wrote stories about fish and the sea for a radio program. Her writing lengthened into several books—*Under the Sea-Wind, The Sea Around Us*, and *The Edge of the Sea.* Then in 1962 she wrote the hard-hitting *Silent Spring* in which she lashed out at the use of chemicals and pesticides which were poisoning the air, the earth, and the sea. Rachel Carson died in 1964—but not before it was clear that her book had stirred Americans to care about saving their environment.

AMELIA EARHART
1897–1937

knew that she had to fly when she
went to her first "air circus" in 1920.
As daredevil airmen swooped and
dived above her in their rickety flying
machines, Amelia had already made
up her mind. She began to take flying lessons not long afterward. Amelia
was called "Lady Lindy" when she
crossed the Atlantic Ocean as one of
a crew of three. The bold young flier
proved that she could do it alone
when in 1932 she became the first
woman to cross the Atlantic. Crowds
cheered her in England; her own
countrymen hailed her at a ticker-tape
parade on Broadway. In 1937 Amelia
started on a daring round-the-world
flight that ended in her mysterious
disappearance. People still wonder
about Amelia Earhart's last flight and
remember her as a pioneer woman
flier—and one of the great fliers of
all time.

Amelia Earhart
Pioneer in the Sky

by *John Parlin*

Copyright © 1962 by John Parlin

First Airplane

Amelia held her younger sister Muriel's hand tightly as the shiny red car in which they were sitting climbed up, up, up to the top of the Ferris wheel. Then, as the wheel turned and the car swooped down, Amelia screamed with delight. Muriel burst into tears.

"There's nothing to be afraid of, Muriel," Amelia said, trying to comfort her sister. "This is fun. It's almost like flying. Look! There's dad down on the ground!"

As the car swung high up over the Iowa State Fair grounds again, the girls could see their father standing far below. He waved to them. Mr. Earhart was pleased that the girls seemed to be having an exciting time.

The Earhart family had lived in Des Moines only a short time. Before that, the girls and their mother had spent a large part of every year with their grandparents in Atchison, Kansas, while Mr. Earhart traveled for the Rock Island Railroad. It was there, in Atchison, that Amelia had been born on July 24, 1898.

Now Edwin Earhart had a better job, and the family could be together all the time. They would have many more outings like this one, he hoped.

The Ferris wheel turned more and more slowly now and finally stopped.

"How was it?" Mr. Earhart asked, as the girls scrambled out of the little car.

"I was scared," Muriel said.

"I wasn't," Amelia bragged.

"Now let's see the airplane," Mr. Earhart said. He had never seen an airplane before. Neither had the girls. They had only seen pictures of airplanes in magazines.

As they walked across the fair grounds, Mr. Earhart talked about airplanes. He told them the Wright brothers had invented the airplane just a few years before. Airplanes were not able to fly very far yet.

Soon they came to a fence. On the other side they saw the airplane.

"It looks like a big orange crate," Amelia said.

"It looks funny," Muriel agreed.

"I thought it would look better than that," Amelia said.

She was disappointed by her first sight of an airplane. She never thought that she would own an airplane when she grew up.

Halley's Comet

One night in 1910, the Earharts were having supper. Mr. Earhart turned to Amelia and Muriel. "Would you girls like to see something exciting tonight?"

"Yes, dad, yes!" Amelia and Muriel shouted together. "What is it?"

"Well," Mr. Earhart said with a laugh, "it has a tail that is several million miles long."

"You're teasing us," Amelia said. "Nothing has a tail that long!"

"I'm not teasing," Mr. Earhart said. "I'm talking about Halley's comet up in the sky." He told them that Halley's comet made a trip near the earth every 76 years. It was named after Edmund Halley, an English scientist who had studied the comet a long time ago.

After they had helped their mother wash the dishes, the girls climbed up on a shed behind the house. Mr. Earhart pointed to Halley's comet.

"It looks like a star with a tail," Amelia said.

"It's not a star," her father said. "We aren't sure exactly what it is. Most scientists think it's made up of millions of small rocks and pebbles."

"I read something interesting about comets the other day," Mrs. Earhart remarked. "Somebody said that a comet is the nearest thing to nothing that anything can be, and still be something."

"Well," said Muriel, "it looks like something to me."

"Isn't it pretty!" Amelia cried.

"Take a good look," Mr. Earhart said. "It will be out of sight in a few days. And it won't come back again until 1986."

Amelia pointed to a bright star near the Milky Way.

"Does that star have a name, dad?" she asked.

"That's Vega," her father replied. "It's one of the most beautiful stars of all."

Amelia shut her eyes and made a wish on Vega. She wished that when she grew up, she could do exciting things.

When they went back in the house, Amelia picked up her favorite cat. "Well, Kitty Cat," she said jokingly, "Halley's comet's tail is a lot longer than yours. You ought to be ashamed of yourself."

Growing Up

The years that followed were happy ones for Amelia. She learned to swim well and to ride a horse. After she finished high school, she studied in Philadelphia. Muriel was going to a school in

Amelia worked as a nurse's aide to help the wounded soldiers of World War I.

Toronto, Canada. During one vacation Amelia went to Toronto to visit Muriel.

In Toronto Amelia saw many soldiers. World War I was being fought in Europe. Canada had been in the war for a long time. Many men had been wounded.

One day Amelia saw four soldiers walking on crutches. She felt sorry for the men. She decided to stay in Toronto.

"I can help these wounded soldiers," she told Muriel.

Amelia became a nurse's aide at a hospital. She

brought medicine and food to the wounded men. The men liked Amelia.

On one of her days off, she and a friend went to an airfield near Toronto. They watched a man do some stunt flying. His daredevil tricks frightened Amelia's friend.

"I can't look," she cried, covering her eyes with her hands.

"Oh, I love it!" Amelia cried. She watched the plane do a somersault in the air. Next the man made his plane roll over. Then he spun down through the sky.

"It's wonderful!" Amelia shouted. "What fun it must be to fly!"

"I wouldn't dare fly," her friend said.

"I would," Amelia said quietly. "And someday I will."

But several years passed before Amelia was able to fly. When the war was over, she went to Columbia University in New York City. She thought she might like to be a doctor. She felt that women could be just as good doctors as men.

Soon Amelia decided that she was not meant to be a doctor. But she could not decide what she wanted to be instead. Her mother and father were now living in Los Angeles, California. So Amelia left Columbia University and went to California.

First Flight

One morning in California, Amelia picked up a newspaper. She read that there was going to be an air meet near Los Angeles. She begged her father to take her. Mr. Earhart liked to see airplanes fly too. So he agreed to go.

In those days fliers often had meets around landing fields. The meets were called "air shows" or "flying circuses." The pilots did lots of stunt flying. Often a brave man jumped out of a plane with a parachute. He made a pretty sight as he floated to the ground.

Amelia was thrilled at the air meet. "I'd like to learn to fly," she said to her father. "I wonder how much it costs."

"Ask that man in uniform over there."

"You ask him for me, dad," Amelia said. "Please! He might think a girl who wants to fly is crazy."

Amelia's father was back in a few minutes. "He said that it costs several hundred dollars!"

"That's a lot of money," Amelia said. "But, dad, I'd . . ."

"You might not like flying, Amelia," her father said hopefully. "You've never even been up."

"Maybe I should go up as a passenger at least once," Amelia said. "If I like it, I'll take lessons."

Mr. Earhart thought Amelia would be frightened on her first flight. But he was wrong. Amelia loved her first flight. The planes in those days did not have glass windows or a roof. They were open to the wind, the rain, and the snow. Before Amelia went up, she put on a flying helmet and some goggles. These were to protect her from the wind. She climbed up on the wing and stepped into the passenger seat.

A man on the ground spun the propeller. That was the way planes were started then. The engine started, and the plane moved down the grassy field. Faster and faster it went.

"Here I go," Amelia said to herself as the plane rose into the sky. A strong wind beat against Amelia's face. She stuck her arm out of the plane. The wind almost tore it off. But Amelia had never loved anything quite so much. As soon as the plane was in the air, she made up her mind to learn to fly.

"I've got to," she said to herself, "no matter how much it costs."

Amelia's father said he could not afford to pay for flying lessons. So Amelia got a job. She used the money she earned to pay her flying teacher.

Her flying teacher was a woman! Her name was

Neta Snook. She was one of the few women in the world who knew how to fly.

Neta taught Amelia how to take off from the ground. She taught her how to bank when she made a turn. She also taught Amelia how to pull out of a dive when the plane stalled.

Finally the day came for Amelia to solo—to go up by herself. Neta Snook had always gone up with her before. Now Amelia would be alone.

Amelia climbed into the plane. She raced it across the field, and it rose into the air. Amelia felt like a bird. But when she brought the plane back to the field, she made a rough landing. Nobody said that she was a good pilot. But at least she had soloed. She had flown alone.

Amelia's mother was proud of her. She helped her buy a small plane. Amelia soon became a good pilot.

"You take to flying like a baby takes to milk," someone said to her. Amelia liked that.

Planes did not fly very high in those days. But Amelia set a women's record for high flying. She flew to 14,000 feet. That's almost three miles high.

Amelia wanted to fly even higher. So she tried again. At 11,000 feet she ran into some thick clouds. There were sleet and snow in the clouds. They stung her face. She couldn't see. She knew she had to get out of the clouds. So she went into a tailspin and dived for the ground. Finally she burst into clear sky beneath the clouds.

When she landed, a man asked her why she had come down in a tailspin.

"It was the fastest way," Amelia said.

"Suppose the clouds had reached all the way to the ground. You would have killed yourself," he said.

But Amelia was not worried. She loved flying more than ever.

"Nothing on sea or land can be more lovely than the realm of clouds," she said.

Neta Snook (left) and her pupil, Amelia Earhart, with an early plane used in flight training

Plans for an Ocean Flight

Amelia had a hard time deciding what she wanted to do. Of course she wanted to fly. She wanted excitement. But she had to earn money too.

At last she found an interesting job at Denison House in Boston. Denison House is a social center. Amelia taught the children in the neighborhood how to play games. She looked after them while their mothers were working.

When Amelia wasn't taking care of the children, she was flying. The children were proud of her.

One day in 1927, Amelia read that Charles A. Lindbergh had flown an airplane from New York to Paris. He was the first man to fly across the Atlantic Ocean alone. It was a great thing to do. Planes then were not nearly so good as planes today. The flight was long and dangerous.

Several women had tried to fly across the Atlantic Ocean, but none had made it. Three young women lost their lives trying.

One day in April 1928, Amelia was called to the telephone.

"Hello, Miss Earhart," a man said. "Would you like to make a long airplane flight?"

Amelia was excited. "Tell me more," she cried.

"I can't tell you over the phone," the man said. "It's a big secret. Come to my office, and I'll explain everything."

When Amelia walked into his office, he seemed pleased with her looks. She was tall and slender and appeared quite at ease. The man thought she looked like Lindbergh.

"How would you like to fly across the Atlantic Ocean?" he asked.

Amelia took a deep breath. "I'd like it," she said.

"If you are chosen, you'll probably just be a passenger," the man said.

"I'd like to be the pilot," she said.

"But you don't know how to use instruments. A man who does will be the pilot."

Instruments could help a pilot tell where he was at all times. They kept him from getting lost when it was dark or foggy. One of the most important instruments was a radio. Instrument flying was new. Amelia had never learned it.

Soon Amelia was sent to New York. There she met George Putnam, a book publisher. He was the manager of the ocean flight.

George and Amelia soon found that they liked many of the same things. And they liked each other. George called Amelia "AE" after her initials. She began calling him "GP" after his initials.

Wilmer Stultz was picked to be the pilot on the ocean flight. Lou Gordon was the flight mechanic. Stultz was a fine pilot, and he knew how to use instruments. Amelia promised herself that someday she would learn instrument flying.

Across the Atlantic

Amelia was pleased when she saw the plane that was chosen for the trip. It was named the *Friendship*. The *Friendship* had three motors. Instead of wheels, it had pontoons. This meant that it could float. It had to take off and land on water.

"I like those gold wings," Amelia said. "They're beautiful!"

"We didn't choose gold because it's a pretty color," Wilmer Stultz laughed.

"No," Lou Gordon said. "That color can be seen a long way off. If we have to come down in the ocean, perhaps we can be rescued."

The men couldn't scare Amelia. She felt sure the *Friendship* would make the flight safely.

In 1928 planes did not fly well in bad weather. It was hard to leave the ground unless the wind was just right. Early one morning the weather seemed right. Amelia and the men climbed aboard the *Friendship*. It was in the waters of Boston harbor.

The engines were started. Seagulls screamed as they heard the roaring motors. The *Friendship* sped across the water. Foam flew like soapsuds beneath it. Slowly the plane rose into the air.

They flew to Trepassy harbor, in Newfoundland, which is off the coast of Canada. There they came down in the water. They planned to fill up again with gasoline, then take off for Europe.

But the weather was bad. Day after day they had fog and rain. Sometimes they tried to take off, but the wind was wrong.

Amelia became discouraged. There was some bad news too. Another young woman had flown from New York to Newfoundland. Her name was Mabel Boll. She was sometimes called "The Diamond Queen" because she wore so much jewelry. Her plane was named the *Columbia*. Mabel and her pilot were now in a town nearby. She hoped to beat Amelia across the Atlantic.

Amelia said it was not a race, and Mabel agreed with her. But of course each wanted to be the first woman to cross the Atlantic by plane.

Back in the United States, the newspapers called it a race. Headlines read:

"Rival Women Fliers Still Held by Bad Weather"
"*Columbia* Ready for Takeoff"
"Weather Delays Both Planes"

With Amelia on board, the *Friendship* (below) arrives at Burry Port in Wales. At Southampton, England she is greeted with flowers.

And finally, in big type, "FRIENDSHIP TAKES OFF"
It was June 17, 1928. Mabel Boll said the weather
was too bad to fly. So if the *Friendship* made it,
Amelia would be the first woman to fly the Atlantic
Ocean.

At first everything went fine. But soon Amelia and
the men ran into heavy fog.

They had hoped to reach Southampton on the
southern coast of England. But after many hours in
the air, they had little gasoline left. If they ran out
of gasoline, they might crash into the sea. Then the
radio stopped working. Without the radio they could
not tell where they were.

But they were lucky. The fog suddenly lifted.
They saw a big ship below. Stultz circled the ship.
Then he wrote a note in which he asked the captain to paint a big sign on the deck. The sign should
tell the fliers where the nearest land was.

Stultz gave the note to Amelia. She tied it in a
bag with an orange to weight it down. Then she
dropped the bag out of the plane. She hoped it
would land on the ship.

It missed! Amelia tried again with another note.
She used their last orange as a weight. She missed
again!

They decided to go on. There was still a chance
of finding land before their gasoline gave out.

A short time later they saw some small fishing boats. They knew that there must be land nearby. But where could it be?

Something blue appeared in the distance. It could be land; or it might be just another cloud. When they came closer to it, they saw that it really was land!

Stultz brought the plane down on the water. They were just off Burry Port, Wales. Both Wales and England are part of Great Britain.

Amelia was the first woman to fly across the Atlantic! She was treated like a heroine. Crowds cheered her wherever she went. Newspapers published stories about her.

The president of the United States, Calvin Coolidge, sent her a message. Mabel Boll sent a nice message too.

Many people compared Amelia to Lindbergh. They called her "Lady Lindy" because, like the great flier, she had flown across the Atlantic. Amelia knew she did not deserve to be called "Lady Lindy."

"I was just a passenger," she said. "I might as well have been a sack of potatoes."

But saying that just made people like her even more. They admired her modesty.

"Someday," Amelia said to herself, "I'm going to fly across the Atlantic all by myself—solo!"

Another Wish upon a Star

Amelia and the two men returned to America. The country gave them a big welcome. There was a parade up Broadway in New York City.

George Putnam asked Amelia to write a book about the flight for his publishing company. The book was called *20 Hrs. 40 Min.* That was how long it took the *Friendship* to fly across the ocean.

When the book was finished, Amelia began flying again. She wanted to get more practice as a pilot. One day she started across the country to California in a small plane.

It was a long flight in those days. She had to stop many times for gasoline. She could not fly at night, for most of the landing fields were not lighted. And there were not many landing fields.

Once she got lost. It was almost dark. Her plane was nearly out of gasoline. Amelia could find no place to land. But she knew she had to land very soon. She circled low over a small town. It had a very wide main street. There were no cars on the street.

"I'll have to try it," Amelia said to herself. She made a fine landing on the main street.

The people who lived there were very surprised! They had never had a visitor from the skies before.

They were proud when they learned that the flier was the famous Amelia Earhart.

"Flying may not be all plain sailing," Amelia said later, "but the fun of it is worth the price."

Amelia returned to New York. She got a job on *Cosmopolitan* magazine. She wrote about flying. She told her readers that many children knew much more about airplanes than grown-ups. She called the children "the flying generation."

Often young people who wanted to learn to fly wrote to Amelia. Many said their parents did not want them to learn. Some told Amelia they took lessons secretly. Amelia thought that was bad. She said that parents should help their children learn to fly.

"The parents should be sure their children learn the *right* way," Amelia said.

When Amelia left the magazine, she worked for a new passenger airline. Her job was to make women like flying. Some women thought flying was not safe. They did not want their husbands to travel by airplane.

Amelia succeeded in making many women think differently about flying.

She also flew a great deal herself. She was becoming a better pilot than ever before, and she was learning to fly with instruments.

Amelia bought a plane called the Lockheed Vega. She remembered the time when she had first seen the star named Vega.

"What a good name for an airplane," she thought. "Maybe I should make another wish."

Amelia wished that she would be the first woman to pilot a plane across the Atlantic—alone!

Atlantic Solo!

"Will you marry me?" George Putnam asked Amelia one day.

"Marriage and flying don't go together," Amelia said.

"But I'll help you with your flying," George said. He finally changed her mind, and soon they were married.

One day Amelia said to her husband, "I'd like to fly across the Atlantic Ocean alone."

George knew the trip would be dangerous. But he had promised to help Amelia with her flying. "If you want to do it," he said, "I'll help you all I can."

Amelia bought a new airplane—another Lockheed Vega. When everything was ready, she flew to Newfoundland. Just after 7 P.M. on May 20, 1932, she took off for Europe—alone.

While Amelia was over the Atlantic, Americans held their breath. Would she make it? Everywhere people prayed that she would.

Amelia did not have an easy flight. Ice formed on her plane's wings. She had to come down close to the sea where the air was warmer. When the ice melted, she climbed again.

Suddenly she saw flames coming from the exhaust pipe. It could mean trouble. The plane might catch on fire. Then a gasoline tank started leaking. It would be terrible if the gasoline caught fire from the exhaust flames.

"I'd rather drown than burn up," thought Amelia. So she brought the plane down close to the waves.

The flames did not seem to get any bigger. So Amelia felt safer. Her plane roared on and on through the night.

The sky slowly grew light. Amelia was hungry. She drank some hot chicken soup from a thermos bottle and ate two chocolate bars. Then she made a hole in a can of tomato juice and drank it.

Amelia had hoped to fly all the way to Paris. But she decided not to risk it. The flaming exhaust pipe and the leaking tank made her change her plans.

She was certainly glad when she saw land ahead. She knew it was Ireland. At last she had flown across the Atlantic alone. Solo!

Amelia Earhart, the first woman to fly solo across the Atlantic, is welcomed in Ireland.

Amelia brought her plane down in a field. It had taken her just fifteen hours and eighteen minutes to fly across the Atlantic. It was a new record.

Soon after she landed, Amelia went to London. A newspaper said, "Not America only, not women only, but the whole world is proud of her."

Amelia was invited to many parties. One night she danced with the Prince of Wales. He would be the king of England when his father died. They talked about flying while they danced.

Afterward someone asked Amelia if the prince was a good dancer. "The prince is a flier and all fliers dance well!" Amelia said.

George Putnam came over by ship to meet Amelia. Together they went to France, Italy, and Belgium. In Belgium they had lunch with the king and queen. Afterward the king gave Amelia a medal.

When Amelia returned to New York, thousands of people cheered her. She received many honors. But Amelia wanted to give some of the credit for her flight to her husband. "It was much harder for him to stay behind than it was for me to go," she said.

American Heroine

Amelia and George were invited to have dinner with President and Mrs. Herbert Hoover at the White House. Afterward they went to Constitution Hall where the president gave her a medal. It was from the National Geographic Society.

"The nation is proud," President Hoover said, "that an American woman should be the first woman in history to fly an airplane alone across the Atlantic Ocean."

Amelia had proved that women have as much courage as men. She was now one of the most famous women alive.

Amelia, who still liked cats, was asked to present a kitten to the Explorers Club in New York City. The kitten, a blue Persian, was to be the club's mascot.

Amelia held the kitten in her arms as she talked to the club members. She told them that there was an old saying about kittens. If you oiled their feet, they would stay home. Perhaps people thought their feet would be too slippery to run away on. So Amelia rubbed oil on the kitten's feet. Then she gave it to the explorers. They named it "Amelia."

Amelia was making many new friends. She was invited to dinner again at the White House. This time her hostess was Mrs. Franklin D. Roosevelt, the new president's wife.

"Would you like to go up in a plane after dinner?" Amelia asked Mrs. Roosevelt.

"I certainly would," Mrs. Roosevelt said. "I have never flown at night."

Amelia arranged for the pilot of a big plane to take them up. George Putnam and some newspaper reporters went with them.

When they were high over Washington, Amelia and the others looked down. They saw the lighted dome of the Capitol building glowing in the darkness. The white shaft of the Washington Monument shone in all its glory.

Amelia went up to the cockpit to speak to the pilot. She had on an evening gown and wore white gloves and slippers. She asked the pilot to let her fly the plane. He gave Amelia his seat.

Back in the cabin a reporter asked Mrs. Roosevelt, "Do you feel just as safe knowing a girl is flying this ship?"

"Just as safe," Mrs. Roosevelt replied. "I'd give a lot to do it myself."

Mrs. Roosevelt said that it really marked a new day in history "when a girl in evening dress and slippers can pilot a plane at night."

"A Challenge to Others"

Amelia became a teacher at Purdue University in Indiana. She taught aviation. The students called her "The Flying Professor."

Purdue gave Amelia an airplane. It was a Lockheed Electra, much bigger than any plane she had ever had.

One night Amelia and George were talking at home. Amelia pointed to a globe map.

"I want to fly all the way around the world," she said.

"Other pilots have done it," George said.

"I know," Amelia said. Then she pointed to the equator on the middle of the globe. "But no one has ever flown around the world at the equator. That's the longest way around."

"And it's the hardest way around," George said.

"Will you help me make my plans?" Amelia asked.

George remembered his promise. "Yes," he said, "you know I will."

One morning in March 1937, Amelia took off from California. Fred J. Noonan was her navigator. Their first stop was Honolulu, Hawaii. They made the flight in less than sixteen hours.

The next day they climbed into the Electra again. As the plane raced down the runway, one of the wings dipped. Amelia tried to right the plane. But she was helpless. The Electra went into a ground loop.

Nobody was hurt. But the plane was a wreck. It had cost $80,000. And it would cost a lot of money to fix it. "But I'm going to have it fixed," Amelia said. "I'm going to try again."

The plane was brought back to California by ship. While it was being repaired, Amelia and Fred Noonan made new plans. They decided to try to fly around the world in the opposite direction. They would still start in California, but they would fly east.

Amelia received hundreds of letters. Many were from boys and girls who wanted to go on the trip.

"I want to see the world," one boy wrote. "I have no money, but I will work my head off." Amelia was sorry she could not take him with her on the long flight.

When the plane was ready, Amelia and Fred flew to Miami, Florida. Here the last plans were made. George Putnam arranged for the right kind of gasoline to be at every place they planned to stop.

On June 1, 1937, Amelia and Fred started around the world again. They flew to South America. They crossed the Atlantic Ocean to Africa. Then they went on to India.

After many days they reached Lae, New Guinea. New Guinea is an island in the Pacific Ocean far across from America.

Amelia and Fred planned to fly to Howland Island next. Howland Island is a tiny speck of land in the middle of the Pacific Ocean. They knew it would be hard to find. If they came down in the ocean, they would probably drown. But they must stop somewhere for more gasoline. And gasoline was waiting for them there.

The United States Coast Guard sent a ship to Howland Island. It was named the *Itasca*. It had a strong radio that could send messages. Amelia hoped that the *Itasca*'s radio could lead her safely to Howland.

On July 2, 1937, Amelia and Fred took off from Lae. They climbed into the sky and flew above the

Amelia checks her equipment and then eases her Lockheed Electra from the runway on the first leg of her final flight.

blue ocean. The *Itasca* tried to reach them by radio. But they were still too far away.

"Have not heard your signals yet," the *Itasca* radioed. "Go ahead. Am listening now."

Amelia did not answer. She probably did not hear the message. Finally Amelia's voice was heard. But there was a lot of noise in the radio. The *Itasca* could not understand what she was saying.

Suddenly Amelia was heard again. She said she was about 100 miles from Howland Island and the ship. She was almost there.

The *Itasca* kept on sending messages. Then suddenly Amelia broke in. She sounded excited and frightened. "We must be on you, but cannot see you," she cried. "But gas is running low."

It was clear to the men on the *Itasca* that Amelia was lost. If she had been where she thought she was, she could have seen the ship.

Then the *Itasca* heard Amelia say, "We are running north and south."

Those were the last words the *Itasca* heard Amelia speak. Amelia never did find the *Itasca* or Howland Island. Her plane must have come down at sea when it ran out of gasoline.

The United States Navy sent many ships and planes to search for Amelia Earhart and Fred Noonan. But they could not find them.

No one knows for sure what happened to Amelia and Fred. Since 1937 there have been many strange stories about their fate. Some people think perhaps the Japanese navy captured them.

All we know for sure is that they disappeared. They probably had to come down in the ocean and were drowned.

Before Amelia left on her dangerous flight, she wrote a letter to her husband. She said that he was to read it only if she were lost.

When all hope for Amelia was gone, George Putnam read the letter. It said:

"I want to do it because I want to do it. Women must try to do things as men have tried. When they fail, their failure must be but a challenge to others."

Amelia's failure was a challenge to others and a help too. She was a pioneer in the sky. The things she learned about flying helped the fliers who came after her. Partly because of the work of Amelia Earhart and Fred Noonan, planes now fly safely over the oceans every day.

Those Magnificent Girls
in Their Flying Machines

Amelia Earhart was not the first American woman flier. From almost the beginning of flight, women have taken to the air with the same daring shown by the early men fliers.

Blanche Scott was the first American woman to make a solo flight. Beautiful Harriet Quimby was the first woman to fly across the English Channel. And Ruth Law and Katherine Stinson performed daring stunts that thrilled the crowds at air meets and fairs.

Then during the thirties, Ruth Nichols, Louise Thaden, Phoebe Omlie, Anne Morrow Lindbergh, and the magnificent Amelia Earhart took the center of the stage. These women and others raced in the Women's Air Derby—soon called the Powder Puff Derby—explored new air lanes, and set altitude, distance, and speed records.

Soon after Amelia Earhart's solo flight across the Atlantic, a young hairdresser named Jacqueline Cochran began to take flying lessons. She was to become the best-known woman flier of her time. During World War II she organized the Women's Air Force Pilots, or WASPS, to test and deliver airplanes for the armed forces.

After the war, Jacqueline Cochran became the first woman to fly across the Atlantic in a jet and the first woman to break the sound barrier. Her career is a link between the trailblazing women fliers of the thirties and the young women fliers of today. These women test planes and enter races—and look forward to the day when they, too, will explore space and fly jet planes for commercial airlines.

Katherine Stinson

THE PIONEERS

Ruth Law

Harriet Quimby

SOME FLIERS OF THE GLORIOUS THIRTIES

Anne Morrow Lindbergh (left) and her famous husband. The Lindberghs flew around the world as a team in the thirties, surveying air routes for the future. Below, Ruth Nichols waves from the cockpit of her airplane after breaking the women's transcontinental speed record in 1930.

TOWARD TOMORROW

Jacqueline Cochran (above), jet pilot and first woman to break the sound barrier. Below, Gini Richardson, winner of the 1971 Powder Puff Derby, is typical of women fliers today. Owner and operator of her own flight school, she won the Derby flying solo.

Index

167

Moses, Lydia (sister of Annie Oakley), 60, 70, 71, 73
Moses, Phoebe Anne. *See* Oakley, Annie
Murphy, Paula, 93 (pics)

N

New York Evening Journal, 52, 53
Newton, Isaac, 116
Nichols, Ruth, 164 (pic)
Noonan, Fred J., 157, 159, 160, 161

O

Oakley, Annie (Phoebe Anne Moses)
   and "Butler and Oakley," 75, 76
   childhood of, 60–61, 62 (pic), 63–64, 65–66, 67–68
   at Coliseum Theater, 74–75
   death of, 89
   becomes "Little Sureshot," 80
   as quail hunter, 68, 69
   and shooting contest with Frank Butler, 71–73
   as shooting teacher, 88–89
   and train wreck, 87–88
   with Wild West Show
      in England, 81–82, 83, 84
      in Germany, 84–85
      and Sitting Bull, 79–80
      as trick shooter, 78 (pic), 79, 83 (pic), 86 (pic)
      in Vienna, 87
Oceanic, 42, 43, 44, 45, 56
Oriental, 43, 44

P

Pacific Bank, 108
Pittsburgh Dispatch, 13, 14, 16, 17, 19, 21
Princess of Wales, 81
Pulitzer, Joseph, 19, 20–21, 22, 29
Pullman Company, 49, 50
Purdue University, 156
Putnam, George Palmer (husband of Amelia Earhart), 143, 149, 151, 154, 155, 156, 157, 161

Q

Quimby, Harriet, 163 (pic)

R

Richardson, Gini, 165 (pic)
Roosevelt, Mrs. Franklin D., 155, 156

S

Seaman, Robert J. (husband of Nellie Bly), 52
Shaw, Joseph (stepfather of Annie Oakley), 68, 70
Sitting Bull, 79, 80
Snook, Neta, 140
Somerville, Mary, 117–118
State of Nebraska, 81
Stein, Joe, 70, 73
Stinson, Katherine, 163 (pic)
Stultz, Wilmer, 144, 147, 148

T

Tolliver, Melba, 55 (pic)
Tom Sawyer, 80
Twain, Mark, 80–81
20 Hrs. 40 Min., 149

V

Van Lawick-Goodall, Jane, 128 (pic)
Vassar College, 119, 120, 122, 123, 125
Vassar, Matthew, 118, 119
Vatican Observatory, 117
Verne, Jules, 37, 38, 39, 41, 46, 48
Victoria, 41, 42
Victoria, queen of England, 81–82, 83

W

Walters, Barbara, 55 (pic)
Welfare Island. *See* Blackwells Island
Whitney, Mary, 122, 124 (pic)
Wild West Show, 77, 79, 81, 85, 87, 88
The World, 9 (pic), 19, 21, 25, 26, 29, 30, 32, 38, 41, 45, 47, 49, 51, 52
World War I, 136
Wright brothers, 133